TH[...]
19[...]

An Anatomy of Loyalist Rebellion

DAVID BOULTON

Torc Books

First published in 1973

Torc Books
published by
Gill and Macmillan Limited
2 Belvedere Place
Dublin 1
and internationally through
association with the
Macmillan Publishers Group

7171 0666 7

Cover designed by Cor Klaasen

Printing history: 5 4 3 2 1

Printed and bound in the Republic of Ireland by
Cahill and Co. Limited
Parkgate Printing Works, Dublin 8

CONTENTS

1 The Other Secret Army 1

2 Ulster's Volunteer Forces 7

3 Origins of the New UVF 23

4 Paisley, Spence and the UVF 34

5 Murder in Malvern Street 48

6 Underground 62

7 The UVF Bombing Campaign 89

8 The Rise of John McKeague 108

9 Enter the UDA 130

10 Realignments 151

11 The Future 184

David Bolton was born in 1935 near London. After an un-successful education he was in turn a clerk, postman, military policeman and journalist, working on the socialist weekly *Tribune* and editing *Sanity*. In 1966 he started writing for television, going on to make his name as one of Britain's lead-ing current affairs TV producer-directors. Since August 1969 he has made eight documentary films on Ireland, including full-length profiles of Ian Paisley and Gusty Spence. His history of conscientious objection, *Objection Overruled,* was published in 1967.

1 THE OTHER SECRET ARMY

If Northern Ireland ever comes to an end, it will be because the protestants started fighting the British.—Lord Craigavon, Ulster's first prime minister, 1922.

It won't be the IRA which will make the position untenable, but the people the army are supposed to be protecting from the IRA.—Roy Hattersley, former Minister of State, Defence, September 1972.

Enjoy this Christmas, it may well be your last in peace. After the New Year you will probably have to organise to resist an imposed solution by the British Government.—John Taylor, former Junior Minister, Home Affairs, Northern Ireland, December 1972.

On the afternoon of 3 January 1973, the first working day of the New Year, the Secretary of State for Northern Ireland, William Whitelaw, gathered his staff together in his Stormont office and proposed a toast 'to a better year than the last bloody year'.

1972, the year of direct rule, had seen the IRA campaign climax, then falter. By Christmas the British army seemed to be holding urban guerilla insurrection to a 'tolerable', if not an 'acceptable', level. But as the IRA threat faded, another had taken its place. 1972 was, above all, the year of the UVF, Ulster's other secret army.

Sixty years earlier, in the name of loyalty to the Crown, a generation of 'loyalists' had armed themselves against the forces of the Crown. Their rifle clubs and drill corps had been unified as the Ulster Volunteer Force. In the winter of 1972-73 an identical insurrection was in course

1

of preparation. And again the name of the Ulster Volunteer Force was on the lips and lapels of loyal rebels.

The letters UVF may be understood in three distinct ways. First, the name of Edward Carson's force founded in 1912 and reorganised as the Ulster Special Constabulary in 1920. Second, as a broad term describing all current manifestations of paramilitary protestantism, including the Ulster Defence Association, Red Hand commando groups, Orange Volunteers, the B Specials Association and even Ian Paisley's Ulster Protestant Volunteers. Third, as the specific organisation calling itself the Ulster Volunteer Force, founded in 1966, led by 'Gusty' Spence and proscribed under the Special Powers Act by Terence O'Neill. This book, as a record and analysis of current events, is about the UVF in the second and third senses.

Spence's UVF is usually described in press reports as 'the secret protestant private army'. Secret it certainly is. By comparison, the IRA – called 'the secret army' by the best of its several historians – is an open book. The leaders of the IRA are household names; members and supporters were, till late in 1972, easily accessible to the inquiring reporter; there is ample documentation. Each wing of the IRA runs its own newspaper and publicity bureau. In contrast, almost nothing of value has been published on the UVF for the good reason that almost nothing has hitherto been known. The UVF publishes no newspaper, runs no publicity bureau. Only Spence himself, among UVF leaders, may be said to be a household name, and since the proscription of his movement he has spent all but a few weeks locked away in Crumlin Road jail. In six years, the number of men who have publicly admitted (or claimed) to be members of the Force has barely reached a dozen. There are good Fleet Street men with their second homes in Belfast's Europa Hotel who have an IRA contact in every catholic ghetto but have never met and talked to a UVF man, and wouldn't know where to

2

begin looking for one. The UVF (for good reason) has never had the attraction for radical intellectuals that the left-orientated Official IRA has. Nor, of course, has it matched the Provisionals in the scale of its warfare and its consequent newsworthiness.

The secrecy surrounding the UVF makes it impossible for a detailed study to be undertaken on the scale of Bowyer Bell's *The Secret Army* or Coogan's *The IRA*. But some painstaking research, undertaken at snatched opportunities in the intervals of a busy working life across the water from Ulster, has made it possible to put together a pencilled profile, if not a full-colour portrait.

I have drawn from a number of sources, all of which must in some degree be qualified. First, I have had a number of meetings and conversations with UVF members and supporters, including Gusty Spence and members of his family. Spence I met and interviewed at length a few days after his 'abduction' while on parole in July 1972. The bizarre circumstances of that meeting are described later. Some of these conversations have been explicitly about the activities and organisation of the UVF, others have been more circumspect. Often I have had no sure way of knowing whether or not I was being told the truth. But the evaluation of information, the sifting of truth from lies, fact from fantasy, is the every-day job of an analytical journalist. Where I have had to rely on guesswork I have made this clear.

Then there are internal documents, distinguished by their extreme rarity. I have had access to some private letters and tape recordings made by Spence in Crumlin Road jail. But the UVF has not turned its minute books over to me.

Official sources are also meagre. The report of the Stormont Committee on Privilege, set up in June 1966 to investigate a UVF threat to Unionist MP Nat Minford, casts useful light on the interconnection between the UVF and movements under Ian Paisley's direct control, before the UVF was proscribed by Stormont and disowned by Paisley. This is a curiously neglected document. The Scarman report, published in April 1972, casts no more than a flicker of light on the UVF bombing campaign of 1969 which helped force O'Neill's resignation. But buried in more than 170 volumes of transcripts of the Scarman hearings, particularly in the lengthy cross-examination of Paisley and John McKeague, are a number of useful clues to UVF activity.

Then there are the court records of trials from 1966 onwards in which acknowledged or alleged UVF members have been involved. In several of these, the men charged made, or were alleged to have made, detailed statements to the police. Some of these statements describe specific UVF actions and generally provide a vivid picture of the internal organisation of the Force. A number were published in the Belfast press during the trial hearings, but many were not. I have not found it easy to persuade the various lawyers involved to let me see the depositions, and in some cases access has been refused. And there is a further difficulty. Considerations of natural justice demand that the use of such documents is heavily qualified. In several instances, for example, prisoners claimed that statements submitted by the prosecution had been forced out of them under duress or simply manufactured by the police. These claims should be borne in mind even where judges and juries have disbelieved them.

Local newspapers have also proved a useful source, particularly of public statements issued in the name of the UVF. But here again there is a problem of evaluation. Since the UVF rarely issues written press statements, but makes its claims and denials by anonymous telephone calls to newsrooms, there is no way of checking their authenticity. The Provisional IRA is known to have formed a black propaganda 'UVF unit' early in 1972, so it is not impossible that some military actions apparently

4

claimed by the UVF have in fact been the work of the Provisionals. Again, the socialist rhetoric of some UVF and UDA statements towards the end of 1972 could indicate either the development of a left tendency within the UVF or the existence of an Official IRA or other Marxist-orientated faction using the UVF's name to inject socialist concepts into the minds of protestant workers. Sometimes there is internal evidence of authenticity. Often there is not.

Finally, a minor source of information has been the IRA itself, first on Spence's activities in jail, where he established a co-operative relationship with some members of the Official IRA, and second on secret talks which took place in July 1971 between the IRA and the UVF.

Much more information is, of course, available about the other paramilitary bodies, distinguished from Spence's UVF by the fact that none of them have yet been proscribed. The largest and most powerful, the Ulster Defence Association, has an open headquarters office and leaders who are readily accessible to press and public. But little, until now, has been published on the origins of the UDA, the role played by the UVF in its formative stages and the literally murderous faction fights which finally determined where power lay within the organisation.

If the profile that follows is sometimes incomplete, there would nevertheless seem to be enough jig-saw pieces available to enable us to understand what the UVF, in its wide and its narrow sense, is about. Such an understanding is urgent. As the first phase of Whitelaw comes to an end in March 1973, an imposed solution draws nearer. The UVF, no less than the IRA, shows every sign of resisting an imposed solution by massive force of arms: Ulster nationalists and Irish nationalists, from their respective slum ghettos in Belfast, joining forces against the soldiers of the Queen.

Many see in such a scenario the ultimate tragedy. But

5

the essence of the tragedy will be that it takes a holocaust to force the realignments which must come if Ireland is to break through to reality. That Ulster has polarised on sectarian lines is tragic. That thousands of 'loyal' protestants have been driven to copy the 'extremism' of the IRA is tragic. But it must be said, or at least whispered, that that is only half the story. The other, brighter, half is that the protestant working class is, through travail, 'catching itself on'. Protestant workers have had a rude and terrible awakening to the fraudulence of 'protestant ascendancy'. They know they have been used, for half a century and much more, by the sleek, slick men of the Unionist Party. Now they have turned on that party and murdered it in cold blood.

The story of the UVF is not just a tale of protestant terrorism. It is also the story of how the protestant working class was forced in extremes to take off on a voyage of self-discovery. It is a voyage that is not yet over – indeed, it is barely begun. But that it *has* begun, and that there can be no going back, is the light shining in Ulster's present darkness.

2 ULSTER'S VOLUNTEER FORCES

When Ian Paisley, Noel Doherty and 'Gusty' Spence formed their Volunteer bodies in 1966 they were following a well-established tradition. The history of protestant law enforcement, official and freelance, is worth a diversionary chapter.

After Pope Adrian IV – the only English Pope in history – sanctioned the Anglo-Norman invasion of Ireland a century after the Norman conquest of England, law and order was maintained at the point of the conqueror's pikes. After the success of the protestant Reformation in England and its failure in Ireland, law enforcement inevitably took on a sectarian character: the catholic Irish were ruled by an ascendant class exclusively protestant.

The sectarian nature of law enforcement intensified when, in the reign of Queen Elizabeth and James I, the best parts of Ireland were 'planted' by English and Scots colonists. The English planters of Munster were Anglican, the lowland Scots and borderers who occupied the east coast of Ulster presbyterian. After the conquest of the seven western-most counties of Ulster in 1603, county Coleraine, re-named Londonderry, was colonised by a consortium of City of London guilds, wholly Anglican, while the rest of the province was divided between Scots and English. It was a condition of settlement that the new landlords be protestant and they bring over with them protestant servants, labourers and craftsmen. They barricaded themselves behind fortifications and enlisted their protestant tenants and employees in armed 'home guard' units. Here was the origin of sectarian paramilitarism. Catholicism, the religion of the 'mere Irish', the natives, was the hallmark of treason and rebellion; protestantism (and particularly Anglicanism) the badge of loyalty to the Crown.

Loyalists had plenty of opportunities to engage rebels, who had an inconvenient tendency to want their lands back and an uncivil inclination to fight for them. Armed bands of protestant militiamen would swoop on the plains from the fortifications, led by captains like Sir James Craig (King James' Clerk of the Wardrobe, granted 1,000 acres in Armagh, ancestor of Northern Ireland's second prime minister), and Sir Arthur Chichester (granted half of county Antrim and most of Belfast, ancestor of both James Chichester-Clark and Terence O'Neill). The pacification of the natives was made a pleasurable diversion as well as a duty. One planter, Sir Thomas Blenerhasset, proposed an annual hunt of catholics:

For an example, the fourth day of March, Lifford, Omagh, they in Fermanagh, Dungannon and Coleraine shall on that day send forth from every one of those places an hundred men; which five hundred men shall as then make search in all, or in all the most suspicious, places. And by being at one instance dispersed with furniture fit for such business, they shall discover all the caves, holes and lurking places of that country, even for an hundred miles compasse. And no doubt it will be a pleasant hunt, and much prey will fall to the followers, for what doth escape will fall to the hands of others, and bring such a terror as the wolf himself will not dare to continue his haunt . . . The charge none, the pleasure much, the profit more . . . Then may we sow, mow, plant, thrive and be merry.

It is not that Englishmen and Scots, protestant by politics rather than religion, were a peculiarly bloodthirsty people. This was the dawning of the age of empire and it became a harsh fact of empire-building – British, Spanish, Portuguese or French – that conquered peoples must needs either submit or be exterminated. These were the standard ethics of imperialism. What distinguished the Ulster model from others was the addition of a sectarian dimension to those of race and culture.

It would also be a mistake to suppose that the protestant community was exclusively aggressive and reactionary, while catholics embodied the liberal virtues. On the contrary, Irish catholicism was dogmatically authoritarian, while the dissenting strains of protestantism were radically democratic. Indeed, when the English civil war came to Ulster, it was the catholic community which fought as 'loyalists' in the king's name, while the presbyterians were the 'rebels'. While Cromwell's armies took a terrible revenge on catholic royalists, they also introduced to Ireland the revolutionary social ideas of the Levellers. Ulster's presbyterians formed the first Irish republican army.

But both their triumph and their radicalism were short-lived. The Restoration saw a purge of dissenters in 'the killing times' and a virtual monopolisation of power by the Anglican gentry. Once the Battle of the Boyne had ensured the Anglican succession, 86 per cent of Ireland was in protestant hands. To keep it that way, the 'penal laws' were enacted and protestant militia armed against the dispossessed catholic majority.

Reduced to mere subsistence on tiny strips of land, rack-rented by absentee landlords, taxed by a protestant parliament and tithed by the Anglican church, the peasants fought back in the only way open to them, through violent secret societies. In night raids on the big estates they wore white hoods over their faces, UDA-style, and were called 'Whiteboys'. Similar oath-bound societies of protestant peasants in Ulster called themselves 'Hearts of Oak' or 'Hearts of Steel'. Such societies were concurrently waging class war throughout Europe. But in Ireland, the issue was again complicated by the religious issue. Where catholic and protestant peasant neighbours competed for land, as, for instance, in parts of Ulster, 'Whiteboys' and 'Oakboys' turned on each other. The common class enemy escaped scot free and any incipient threat of revolution was nipped in the bud.

Revolution, when it came, came in America. The British troops which had occupied Ireland since Elizabethan times were suddenly withdrawn for transatlantic service, leaving the protestant colonies dangerously exposed. The emergency was met by the mass enrolment of 'Volunteer' corps all over the country and particularly in Ulster. By 1779 40,000 men had been enrolled into corps which bore such names as the Boyne Company, the Glorious Memory Battalion and the True Blues. This first Ulster volunteer force gave the outnumbered colonists, in matters of security, a sense of self-reliance and self-sufficiency they were never to lose.

In country areas, many Volunteer corps remained exclusively protestant and 'loyalist'. In Belfast matters were more complex. Presbyterians and other dissenters, excluded from a political power monopolised by the Anglican gentry, had turned to commerce and now formed a new, wealthy middle class. In Dublin, similarly excluded catholics, driven to trade, had formed a parallel bourgeoisie. The new class in both cities was beginning to demand its proper share of legislative and administrative power and joined together in a campaign for radical parliamentary reform and free trade. Many of the new liberals, influenced by the writings of Tom Paine and later fired by the French revolution, began to flirt with republican ideas. Some were to join Wolfe Tone's Society of United Irishmen, pronouncing religious differences outmoded and irrelevant.

These middle-class radicals wanted power for the middle class: a limited aim, but a distinct advance on a system in which political power was wielded exclusively by the aristocracy. Very few envisaged an extension of democracy to the rural peasants or the emerging urban working class who formed the rank and file of the Volunteer corps. But the corps soon took on the political colours of their officers. Belfast corps, officered by the new middle class, went radical and even admitted some catholics. The country corps, officered in the main by the Anglican aristocracy, stayed conservative and exclusively protestant.

Inevitably the ruling class – the Anglican gentry who monopolised the Irish parliament – saw the threat posed to their ascendancy by the new liberalism of commercial Belfast, and took to the counter-revolutionary barricades. Their fears were articulated by an MP named George Ponsonby:

There are in this country two sets of men who are interested in promoting a change—the catholics of the south, the known friends to monarchy, and the presbyterians of the north, the votaries of republicanism. These latter have set on the others to make it a common cause, and between them both, the established church is blockaded; but if the people who have established the constitution shall be overpowered by those who often attempted to destroy it, we shall have them quarrelling among themselves for votes, for seats in parliament, for authority and supremacy.

A judicious mixture of concession, repression and plain trickery prevented the cementing of middle-class unity across religious barriers and the Lord Lieutenant was able to write with satisfaction to London: 'The terror of the papists begins to operate, the dissenters have caught the alarm, and these jarring parties may perhaps from jealousy become the instruments of peace and good government.'

In rural Ulster, sectarian warfare now broke out with renewed vigour. Protestant groups calling themselves 'Peep o' Day Boys' began dawn raids on catholic homes, ostensibly in search of firearms. Despite the arming of catholics accepted into the Volunteers, the penal law forbidding catholics to bear arms was still on the statute books. The 'Peep o' Day Boys' took the law into their own hands, carrying out their searches in the name of protestant law and order. Frequently they met with resistance.

11

Presbyterians too, as suspected subversives, sometimes attracted the attention of the 'Peep o' Day Boys'. After a series of skirmishes in Armagh in 1784, victims of these raids organised a 'Defender' group which was predominantly catholic but led by a presbyterian minister. Having inflicted initial defeat on a 'Peep o' Day' gang in the village of Nappach, the Defenders managed for a time to impose a catholic leader on the 'Nappach fleet'. But the arrangement didn't last long. The Defenders were soon exclusively catholic, the 'Peep o' Day Boys' exclusively protestant. The dawn raids escalated to a terrorism designed to drive all catholics out of Ulster. Catholic looms were smashed, furniture hacked to pieces, homes fired. Sectarian guerilla warfare was to rage throughout rural Ulster for another ten years.

After a particularly violent battle in September 1795 at a hamlet called The Diamond, in Armagh, the victorious faction of 'Peep o' Day Boys' and other protestants formed the Orange Order. Within a year the Order numbered several thousand members in ninety local lodges.

Against this unpromising background of sectarian civil war in the countryside, Wolfe Tone staged his United Ireland insurrection. It was defeated by a combination of uniformed and freelance protestant force. First, the politically suspect (because integrated) Volunteer corps were disbanded and replaced by a new Yeomanry, exclusively protestant and recruited by the big landowners. Second, the new and rapidly growing Orange Order was enrolled as a kind of special constabulary to assist the authorities. A recruiting officer for the Yeomanry described how he made sure of enrolling only proved 'loyalists': 'By taking into counsel a number of the Orange leaders, deciding to select a certain proportion from each lodge, the thing was well managed.'

The gentry were quick to see the value of the lodges. Writing when the Order was barely a year old, a Dun-

12

gannon magistrate noted their usefulness and incidentally coined a metaphor which Lord Randolph Churchill was to pick up with devastating effect a century later: 'As for Orangemen, we have a rather difficult card to play; they must not be entirely discountenanced; on the contrary, we must in a certain degree uphold them, for with all their licentiousness, on them we must rely for the preservation of our lives and properties should critical times occur.'

Sectarian hatreds were deliberately fostered. As the Yeomanry proceeded to disarm the rebels, a brigadier reported from Dungannon: 'I have arranged a plan to scour a district full of unregistered arms, and this I do, not so much with a hope to succeed to any extent, as to increase the animosity between Orangemen and the United Irish. Upon that animosity depends the safety of the centre counties of the north.' And the same officer noted the political potential of Orangeism: 'If government is resolved to resist catholic emancipation, the measure of adding strength to the Orange party will be of the greatest use.'

By mid-1798 the original proletarian leadership of the lodges had been almost entirely displaced by gentry, and a generation later the Tory bloc of peers were virtually all Orange masters. The old landowning classes, in England as well as Ireland, saw the peasant rank and file of the Order as an instrument providing muscle for their own factional purposes, while the lodges gave the protestant peasant an outward and visible assurance that, despite the lowly station to which God was pleased to call him, he nevertheless had a part in the ruling ascendancy. Economically he might be little better off than his catholic neighbour: no less exploited, taxed, tithed and rack-rented. But, like a later generation of poor whites in America, he had the consolation of knowing there was always someone worse off than himself. If he shared nothing else with the gentry in the big houses, the common rhetoric of the lodges gave him an illusion of equality. Their victory at the Boyne was his victory, their responsibility to uphold protestant law and protestant order was his responsibility. So he took from the old Volunteers the celebration of protestant victories with interminable processions and arcane regalia : an outward and visible sign of his ascendancy over the natives.

After the suppression of the United Irish rising, Westminster abolished the subsidiary Irish parliament and instituted direct rule. The catholics had to wait another twenty-five years for the first stage of their political emancipation, and longer before they were strong enough to begin a serious campaign for the return of home rule. Both developments provoked Orange revivals. By the 1830s the continuing sectarian warfare of the countryside began to be imported into Belfast as first the linen, then the shipbuilding industries attracted labour to the city from surrounding villages. Catholic and protestant newcomers settled in communities around their own churches, and working-class Belfast was quickly divided into sectarian ghettos. After the 1835 celebration of the Battle of the Boyne, a riot developed between the protestants of Sandy Row and the catholics of the Markets area. Several rioters were sabred by the military and two were shot dead. Modern Belfast was born.

The long series of commissions of enquiry which led to Cameron and Scarman more than a century later began after a particularly vicious outbreak of communal rioting in 1857. The commissioners observed that

The Orange system seems to us to have no other practical result than as a means of keeping up the Orange festivals and celebrating them, leading as they do to violence, outrage, religious animosities, hatred between classes and, too often, bloodshed and loss of life . . . We feel a hope that when the kindly and generous minds belonging to the Orange Society see the results attending this organisation—so different from what they intended—they will think that it is well to consider whether there is any controlling necessity to keep it alive.

One aspect of the 1857 situation which has a familiar ring was the prohibition of catholic gun clubs while protestant clubs were allowed to flourish. Another was the partisan role of the Belfast Town Police. Of its 160 constables, 155 were protestants. They were commanded by a seventy-seven-year-old veteran named Adam Hill, who claimed to be a founder-member of the Orange Order. Hill's police career had survived a conviction for corruption in the 1841 general election when he was agent for the Belfast Conservative Party. The commission of enquiry found the force 'undisciplined, partisan and suspected by all decent inhabitants . . . Instead of being a help they become a hindrance'.

The primary political problem for the ruling class throughout the nineteenth century was how to hold on to power in face of the threat posed by the rise of democracy and the extension of the franchise. In England, the first industrial society, the threat of revolution was met by giving the working class a controlled share of the loot pouring in from exploitation of the Empire. In Ireland, it was met by maintaining sectarian divisions. The Orangeman was the conscious and willing ally of the ascendancy class, loyally opposing every political development which threatened its power. For this loyalty he expected some reward.

When the Queen's ministers at Westminster announced their conversion to Irish home rule, the Orangemen felt betrayed. Both Gladstone and Disraeli calculated that concession rather than repression would prevent revolution in Ireland. Both pursued policies which, within the span of a single generation, converted Ireland from a nation of land-hungry and therefore revolutionary peasants to a nation of small farmers occupying their own land: the most conservative class of all. Gladstone went further. Hitherto the argument against home rule or a Fenian republic hinged on the evident danger of Britain having a revolutionary, and therefore unfriendly, offshore island as her neighbour. But Gladstone perceived that, with revolution averted, a limited measure of home rule would no longer threaten Britain's security. The Orangemen had always been used as a counter-revolutionary force. Now the success of counter-revolution made them expendable.

With traditional loyalties so violently overturned, the Orange Order became the focal point of resistance to British policy. The gentry's connections with the Order had weakened latterly, but now the upper classes came scurrying back to their ever-present help in time of trouble. Wrote Lord Cushendun, himself an Orangeman:

Large numbers of country gentlemen, clergymen of all protestant denominations, business and professional men, farmers and the better class of artisans in Belfast and other towns joined the lodges, the management of which passed into capable hands; the society was thereby completely and rapidly transformed and, instead of being a somewhat disreputable and obsolete survival, it became a highly respectable as well as an exceedingly powerful organisation.

The Westminster politician who most clearly recognised the potential of militant Orange unionism was Lord Randolph Churchill, an Independent Conservative whose 'Tory-democrat' (today we would call it populist) philosophy was based on the conviction that Toryism had no future unless it could find ways of detaching a major segment of the working class from Liberal and Lib-Lab connections. Churchill recognised in Orangeism, as Enoch Powell was to do nearly a century later, an authentic expression of 'Tory democracy', and he determined to 'play the Orange card'. He warned a Belfast rally that home rule was 'coming upon them like a thief in the night', but 'in that dark hour there will not be wanting to you those of position and influence in England who are willing to cast in their lot with you'. Thus the weight of English Toryism was thrown behind the unionist-Orange cause. As the first home rule Bill came before parliament, arrangements were formally put in hand for the merging of all anti-home-rule groups in a Unionist Party directly linked to the Westminster Conservatives and based on the grass-roots organisation of the Orange Order. As Lord Cushendun noted, the Order's 'system of local lodges, affiliated to a Grand Lodge in each county, supplied the ready-made framework for an effective organisation'. Henceforth the Orange Order and the Unionist Party were different facets of a single, integrated force.

There was also an upsurge of freelance organisation. Scores of Unionist rifle clubs were established, providing a legal framework for arms training. A Belfast 'Vigilance Committee' placed an order for '20,000 Snider rifles in good order, with bayonets'. And a presbyterian minister known as 'Roaring Hanna' roared: 'Every capable loyalist should be enrolled in a loyal defensive union to meet any emergency which may arise. Let captains of hundreds, captains of fifties and captains of tens be elected and their corps constructed to meet the danger.'

The first home rule Bill failed because of a Liberal split. When Gladstone made his second attempt in 1893, Unionism was organised and armed to resist it. This time a young Belfast engineer, Fred Crawford, augmented constitutional resistance by founding a secret society, 'Young Ulster'. According to a modern defender of the Unionist position,

A condition of membership of this society was the possession of one or another of three weapons, a revolver, a Martini-Henry rifle or a cavalry Winchester carbine, together with a hundred rounds of ammunition. As the Arms Act was in force the members had to prepare their ammunition secretly, melting their lead into bullet moulds in the heating furnaces of certain presbyterian churches.

Gladstone's second Bill was defeated by the Conservative and Unionist majority in the Lords and not until the Lords' power of veto had been abolished could a third attempt be made at home rule, in 1912. This time, armed resistance in Ulster was on a much greater scale than ever before.

It was led by a Dublin lawyer, Edward Carson. 'We must be prepared,' he told a rally of 50,000 Orangemen in Belfast, 'the morning home rule passes, ourselves to become responsible for the government of the protestant province of Ulster.' To give effect to this threat of UDI, a 'provisional government' was formed with Carson at its head. Bonar Law pledged the support of the British Conservative Party. There were, he said, 'no lengths of resistance to which Ulster can go in which I should not be prepared to support them'.

That summer Unionist magistrates began licensing Orange lodges all over Ulster to drill and train what amounted to Orange private armies. By the end of 1912, these bodies had been drawn together as a unified Ulster Volunteer Force.

Recruiting was done essentially by the Orange Order . . . as the Lodge room was no hiding place for conscientious objectors or political opportunists. Likewise, drilling was carried on in the Orange Halls, but when the weather and landowners permitted, drilling was done openly . . . The UVF were given a suite of offices in the Belfast Town Hall, where the (provisional) government sat . . . Belfast businessmen underwrote the UVF to the tune of £1 million.—['Carson's UVF', *Protestant Telegraph,* 30 Jan. 1971.]

As with the Volunteers of a century earlier, the gentry in the countryside and the businessmen in the towns took commissions in the UVF and recruited their tenants and employees. Rifles were imported from England, and sympathetic British army officers – of whom there was no shortage – were recruited to positions of command. It was claimed that UVF drilling was legal, since it was licensed by local magistrates, often themselves UVF officers. Carson knew better: 'Drilling is illegal,' he conceded, 'the Volunteers are illegal and the government know they are

18

illegal, and the government dare not interfere with them. . . Don't be afraid of illegalities.'

The UVF grew to 90,000 men, financed by the Belfast business community and by highly placed supporters in England and the empire. Rudyard Kipling gave £30,000 and a poem, 'Ulster 1912'. Lord Rothschild, Lord Iveagh and the Duke of Bedford gave £10,000 each. These funds were used to equip the UVF professionally with guns purchased in European markets. Gun-running continued on a massive scale even after Asquith belatedly made all importations of firearms illegal in 1913.

In April 1914, in an exploit which now ranks second only to the Boyne in protestant mythology, the UVF's arms organiser, Major Frederick Crawford, landed at Larne harbour a cargo of no less than 35,000 rifles and 3,000,000 rounds of ammunition, bought in Germany and smuggled in under the noses of the British navy. Believing at an early stage of the hazardous sea journey that the cargo was about to be intercepted by customs men, Crawford (the same who had founded the secret armed organisation 'Young Ulster' in the 1890s) called for divine intervention.

I walked up and down the deck, tormented by the thought of all those men waiting for me to bring them the weapons with which to fight for their religion, their liberty and all that was dear to them . . . I went into my cabin and threw myself on my knees, and in simple language told God all about it: what this meant to Ulster, that there was nothing sordid in what we desired, that we wanted nothing selfishly. I pointed out all this to God, and thought of the old psalm, 'O God our help in ages past, our hope for years to come'.— (Quoted by A.T.Q. Stewart, *The Ulster Crisis*.)

Having had the situation explained to him, God guided the boat safely home, where its cargo transformed the UVF into a formidable army.

While Crawford and God between them were bringing

19

in the sinews of rebellion, the British War Office was planning a military move against the UVF. But the officers of the 3rd Cavalry Brigade at the Curragh, near Dublin, refused to move against pro-British Ulster. The UVF won its first engagement without firing a shot.

The home rule Bill continued its stormy passage through parliament, passing its final stage on 8 September 1914. By that time Britain had been at war with Germany for a month and the operation of home rule was delayed until after the war. Protestant Ulster was bitter at what it saw as a mere stay of execution for the domestic convenience of the executioner. Police intelligence reported from Belfast

. . . a very bitter feeling on the part of the Unionists against the government for passing the Bill and against His Majesty for signing it. This was shown by the disrespect with which His Majesty's picture was greeted at picture houses, and by the action of members of the congregation at several protestant churches in walking out during divine service when the national anthem was being sung.

Protestant loyalty to the Crown was clearly dependent on the Crown's loyalty to protestants.

The German war posed a cruel dilemma for the UVF, which had armed itself with German guns to fight the British and had actually been soliciting the political backing of the Kaiser – 'Europe's most powerful protestant monarch' – when war broke out. Now it was asked to place its men and its arms at the disposal of the British War Office. After some hesitation, Carson allowed his force to be incorporated into Kitchener's army as the 36th (Ulster) Division. Carson himself, despite his recent history of rebellion, was co-opted into Britain's war cabinet. Then, in July 1916, the UVF was virtually wiped out in the mud of the Somme. It was said that on their last advance against the German trenches they were still shouting 'No surrender!'

But the UVF had given birth to imitations. In the south

20

of Ireland, Carson's actions were copied by the founders of the Citizen Army and the Irish Volunteers. Their militants did not join the British army. Instead, they launched the abortive insurrection of Easter 1916. A new tide of nationalism and republicanism swept the south in the wake of the execution of the rebellion's leaders, and when the German war was over Britain found itself faced, not with a threatened protestant coup in Belfast but with the reality of a catholic UDI in Dublin, defended in arms by the Irish Volunteers, renamed the Irish Republican Army.

The forces sent to attempt to restore protestant and British law and order now took the form of a para-military force recruited in England from the unemployed. Dressed in a hastily assembled mixture of police black and army khaki, they were nick-named the 'Black-and-Tans'. While they engaged the IRA in the south, what amounted to a revived UVF tackled the same job in the north.

Early in 1920 Lloyd George approved the reorganisation of the UVF as the Ulster Special Constabulary. Later that year the Government of Ireland Act partitioned the country and gave six counties of Ulster their own provincial parliament. The 'Specials' immediately assumed a crucial paramilitary role. So widespread was the arming of 'loyalists' and the swearing-in of 'Specials' that official reports indicate that the strength of the police from 1921 to 1926 'cannot be stated'. (A and B Specials were properly accounted for, but the part-time reserve of C Specials was of unknown numbers. The C men were never formally disbanded but just allowed to fade away. Where their weapons faded to is a matter for speculation.) The Specials were permitted to carry their arms even when off duty and in plain clothes, a privilege which lasted till their transformation into the Ulster Defence Regiment in 1969. For fifty years they played the role of Unionism's private army.

The planters' home guards, the Volunteers of the 1780s, the Yeomen, 'Peep o' Day Boys' and Orangemen of the 1790s, the rifle clubs and 'Young Ulster' at the end of the nineteenth century, the UVF of 1912 and the USC of the last fifty years: these are the varied forms taken by Ulster's paramilitary protestantism. All have professed a fanatical devotion to the British Crown, the British constitution, the British way of life: and all have been prepared to fight Britain to stay British.

Such is the profile of rebel loyalism. The Paisleys and Spences of Ulster have a long lineage.

3 ORIGINS OF THE NEW UVF

At the end of June 1966 Captain Terence O'Neill, fourth
prime minister of Northern Ireland, flew to France to
celebrate *in situ* the fiftieth anniversary of the slaughter
of the old UVF on the banks of the Somme. His visit was
suddenly cut short. Telephoned by his cousin, Major
James Chichester-Clark, he hurried home to a domestic
crisis. Next day he declared the new UVF an illegal
organisation. It was the only protestant group to share
that distinction with the IRA.

O'Neill was used to crises. Northern Ireland had permanent crises as China had permanent revolution. After
the crisis which gave birth to the statelet there were the
successive crises of wholesale unemployment through the
late 'twenties and 'thirties, then the crisis of a renewed
IRA campaign in 1939, then that of European war in
which Ulster was the only part of the United Kingdom
to have a land frontier, then the crisis of Unionist adjustment to Labour's post-war welfare state, then that of the
IRA border campaign of 1956-62.

But O'Neill presided over a crisis of adjustment greater
than all these. When he took over from Lord Brookeborough in 1963 the post-war economic boom was fading.
The Belfast aircraft industry had lost its war market,
the shipyards were at half capacity and the old linen
industry, the foundation of Ulster's wealth, was threatened
by cheap synthetic fibres. A major depression would
follow unless the province's economic base was dramatically overhauled.

Overhaul meant massive redeployment to new growth

industries. But this posed a dangerous problem for traditional Unionism. The old contracting industries were those in which the protestant working class enjoyed a clear ascendancy over catholic workers. In the shipyards, for instance, Belfast's largest single source of employment, more than 90 per cent of the jobs were held by protestants. Unionist power depended on the party's ability to hold the loyalty of the protestant working class, and that loyalty was strictly a *quid pro quo* for institutionalised discrimination and preference in employment. So the Unionist leadership faced a critical dilemma: failure to modernise meant inevitable economic decline and mounting unemployment, while modernisation threatened disruption of the complex system of patronage by which Unionism bonded together conflicting class interests.

With O'Neill at the helm, the impetus of economic rationalisation quickened. He promoted a policy of encouraging overseas investment in Ulster by offering financial inducements to overseas firms to open factories in the province. Many did so, only to pull out when the concessionary tax-free period ran out, causing high localised unemployment. Moreover, the demands of this kind of fly-by-night industry for cheap, often unskilled, labour, favoured catholic workers (and women). The protestant aristocracy of labour increasingly felt its security threatened.

O'Neill thought he could ignore these fears and hold the Unionist Party together by the force of his own personality. He showed no sign of understanding the nature of the link between the protestant working class and the ascendant class from which he himself came. O'Neill's pedigree stretched back to the Ulster plantation. He was descended from Arthur Chichester, the colonial conqueror of Ulster, through a line which had taken the O'Neill name (and part of the O'Neill estates) in the nineteenth century. He was a product of Eton and the

Irish Guards, with the manners, accent and outlook of the British ruling class. His lofty paternalism never found better expression than in his observation that 'if you treat Roman Catholics with due consideration and kindness they will live like Protestants'. O'Neill was essentially an English gentleman and he sought to emphasise those aspects of Unionism reflecting the traditions of English Toryism and play down those which were peculiar to Ulster.

The single event which both symbolised O'Neill's revised version of Unionism and highlighted the discontent of traditional Unionists was the visit to Belfast of the prime minister of the Irish Republic, Seán Lemass, in January 1965. He came at O'Neill's invitation for talks on 'economic co-operation', and O'Neill assured his cabinet colleagues, whom he had not bothered to consult in advance, that there was no question of any discussion of the constitution. Nevertheless, to those who, under Unionist tutelage, had learned to regard the Republic as an enemy state and Lemass as a puppet of the Pope, O'Neill was henceforth suspect as at best an appeaser and at worst a traitor.

In the wake of this traumatic event, Ulster was plunged into the past as the Republican movement announced plans for a series of public celebrations of the fiftieth anniversary of the 1916 rising. Fears of renewed IRA activity were given official backing when Home Affairs Minister Brian McConnell told Stormont he had evidence of a new IRA campaign of subversion. The start of 1966 was a tense time in Ulster.

Unionists were also stepping out into the past. Controversy raged over the name for a new bridge across the Lagan, just completed by Belfast corporation. Traditional Unionists wanted to call it Carson Bridge and opposed the Governor's suggestion that it be called Queen's Bridge, Carson evidently out-ranking the Queen on the 'loyalists' ' roll of honour.

1916, renewed talk of IRA subversion – and Carson. It made an explosive mixture for Belfast. Turmoil among traditional Unionists now began to focus on three men: Ian Paisley, Noel Doherty and Augustus ('Gusty') Spence.

Paisley was a crude but effective bible-thumper after the manner of 'Roaring Hanna' and a long line of spiritual recruiting sergeants for traditional Unionism. He was born in Armagh in 1926, the son of an Independent Baptist pastor who had served in Carson's UVF and in 1928 opened his own gospel 'station' in Ballymena. At the age of eight, according to his mother, the favourite reading of the young Paisley was a tome called *Death of Deaths,* a guide to hell and how to avoid going there. At sixteen he went to the Barrie School of Evangelism in Wales, renowned for its piety rather than its learning. A year later he switched to the Theological Hall of the Reformed Presbyterian Church, Belfast, from which he obtained a certificate saying he was 'highly recommended as a student and preacher of the Gospel'.

Leaving college in 1945, he promptly founded a National Union of Protestants, with himself at the head, and started a paper, *The Protestant,* with himself as editor. The paper lasted only a few issues. Much more durable was his relationship with the Ravenhill Evangelistic Mission, a run-down gospel hall near the shipyards in East Belfast. Paisley accepted a 'call' to be pastor there, then arranged to have himself ordained in a ceremony presided over by his father and other fundamentalist ministers.

Following his twenty-first birthday, the Rev. Ian Paisley joined the Orange Order and was appointed chaplain to the Junior Orangemen. He also began to appear on Unionist Party platforms. On 12 July 1949 he shared a platform with Brian Faulkner, who at twenty-eight had just become the party's youngest MP. Faulkner moved a resolution asserting 'the clamant need to resist the unscrupulous attempts of communism to seduce our people', and attacked Attlee for approving Eire's change of name to 'the misleading and absolutely deceptive title "Republic of Ireland" '. Paisley's contribution is unrecorded.

But Paisley's primary activity was gospel campaigning, often in presbyterian church halls. During one such campaign in Crossgar, county Down, early in 1951, his preaching split the congregation and a breakaway 'Free Presbyterian Church' was formed in a local Orange Hall. More splits followed and the resultant new churches formed the Free Presbyterian Church of Ulster with Paisley as Moderator, a post he was to hold continuously to the present day except for one short break when poor health forced a temporary retirement.

Paisley attacked the theological liberalism of the official presbyterian church and boasted that while presbyterianism had quietly abandoned embarrassing old doctrines such as hell and damnation and the blood sacrifice of Christ, he continued to stand by them, however unfashionable. In particular, he attacked presbyterianism's support for the new ecumenical movement which had as its goal the ultimate reunion of all the Christian churches – including Rome.

The ecumenical controversy had special relevance to Northern Ireland. The great mass of people calling themselves protestants neither knew nor cared that the leadership of their churches had long abandoned classical Calvinism and the bible fundamentalism associated with the Reformation. The shipyard worker and the shirt factory operator knew little and cared less about arcane theological distinctions separating fundamentalist from modernist. The significance of the ecumenical movement was that it made the difference evident in political terms : those who preached ecumenism – and they included the leaders of all the major churches organically linked to the ruling political elite – were selling out to Rome. Those who preached fundamentalism were making a stand for 'traditional Unionism'. This was one of the major objective factors behind the rise of Ian Paisley. For in Ulster, ecumenism carried a threat of catholic integration, a threat to protestant ascendancy and privilege in jobs, housing and access to political power.

Paisley's first taste of notoriety came in 1956. A week after his wedding to a young sister in the Plymouth Brethren on 13 October, a fifteen-year-old catholic girl from the Falls Road disappeared. Her name was Maura Lyons and it transpired that she had secretly joined Paisley's church four days before her disappearance. After her family reported her missing, rumours began to circulate that she had been 'kidnapped' by the Free Presbyterians. One of Paisley's ministers, Rev. David Leatham, admitted to the police that she had been at his house on the night of her disappearance, but volunteered no information on her subsequent whereabouts. Paisley's assistant Moderator, Rev. John Wylie, had his home searched, and organised with Paisley a rally in the Ulster Hall to protest against 'police brutality'.

Paisley caused a sensation when he publicly announced that the rally would feature 'a message from Maura Lyons'. It took the form of a tape-recording which Paisley claimed to have found on his doorstep one morning. The girl told of her 'conversion' and said she had run away because her parents had wanted to put her in a convent. Paisley told the rally he would never hand any girl over to the Church of Rome. 'The police say "You are committing an offence." Very well, I am committing an offence. I will do time for it. I would be proud to do time for protestant liberty.'

Six months later, on the girl's sixteenth birthday, Paisley called the police to tell them she had arrived at his home asking him to protect her. Ten days later she was made a ward of court. Paisley and Wylie were expressly forbidden access to her by Lord Chief Justice McDermott, who censured Paisley for refusing to give evidence. There were people present, said the judge, 'who must have been party to that abduction and who at least must have aided and abetted . . . If evidence can be found against them, I hope the Attorney-General will direct a prosecution'.

There was no prosecution, but Paisley's notoriety was now established. It was consolidated when, two years later, he was fined £5 for causing a breach of the peace at an open-air meeting addressed by Dr Donald Soper in Bally-mena. Paisley refused to pay and told his sorrowing congregation: 'Across me lies the shadow of two months' imprisonment.' But he was robbed of martyrdom by an anonymous donor who paid the fine 'in the interests of Unionist unity'.

Unionist unity was no longer of much concern to Paisley. He had quarrelled with the leadership earlier in 1959 when Brookeborough refused to expel two MPs who suggested that party membership should be open to 'catholic Unionists'. Paisley seriously considered fighting East Belfast in the 1959 Westminster general election as an Independent Unionist sponsored by a body called Ulster Protestant Action. UPA, in which he played a leading role, was organised 'to keep protestant and loyal workers in employment in times of depression, in preference to their catholic fellow-workers'.

In the event, he waited another five years before putting his popularity to the electoral test, and then only by fielding four 'Protestant Unionist' candidates in the Belfast corporation elections. But Paisleyism was a movement of the streets, and it was in the streets that it demonstrated its strength in violent rioting during the 1964 general election. Paisley brought thousands of his followers out in protest against the display of an Irish tricolour at a Republican candidate's headquarters in Divis Street, forcing the RUC to take action to remove the illegal flag when they would clearly have preferred to ignore it. Their raid led to two days of sectarian rioting in which thirty people, including eighteen policemen, went to hospital. The Unionist candidate, James Kilfedder, went on to win the seat and embarrassed his leaders by publicly thanking Paisley, 'without whose help it could not have been done'.

In the meantime, Paisley had been busy trying to acquire academic respectability. Back in 1954 he had set about obtaining some degrees and a set of imposing letters to put after his name. He acquired by post a BD and an honorary DD from an American outfit calling itself the Pioneer Theological Seminary at Rockford, Illinois – an institution listed by the US Department of Higher Education as a 'bogus degree mill'. He paid a subscription to the Royal Geographical Society, which entitled him to put FRGS after his name. He also became a member of a 'Royal Society of Literature' (MRSL) and a Fellow of a 'Philosophical Society of Great Britain' (FPLS). In 1958 he obtained an MA from another American institution, Burton College, Colorado, described by the US as 'perhaps the most infamous of all the degree mills'. All these 'degrees' were obtained by mail order: contrary to popular legend, he never studied in America. Not till 1966 did he drop these spurious distinctions in favour of an honorary DD awarded by the Bob Jones University of Greenville, Carolina, a racist bible-belt institution which has also honoured Billy Graham, George Wallace and Barry Goldwater. Like the other bodies from which Paisley obtained his degrees, Bob Jones lacks any official accreditation as an educational establishment. According to an American profile, its rules

. . . forbid all students to see any Hollywood movies, smoke, drink, dance, wear any 'immodest dress, such as tight pants', attend Billy Graham rallies, talk to any strangers, especially newsmen, make any use of jazz, singing or listening to, play cards, leave the campus after 10.30 p.m., use the gym, tennis courts or swimming pool in sexually mixed groups, have dates off the campus without special permission or chaperones, or have dates on the campus for more than two hours. Whether sitting or standing, couples must always keep a six-inch space between their bodies.

Paisley never lacked devoted followers, some the weak and wanting minds which every colourful and assertive form of revivalist religion attracts, others altogether harder men drawn by the violence of the preacher-politician's rhetoric. One man who was probably in the first category was Noel Doherty.

As a young printer's apprentice of fifteen, Doherty had joined Paisley's church in 1956. Thereafter he played an increasingly prominent role, first in the church and later in such movements as Ulster Protestant Action. In 1964, when he was still only twenty-three, Paisley selected him as one of four 'Protestant Unionist' candidates contesting Belfast corporation seats – the first time Paisleyism gave itself a party label and entered electoral politics. Doherty failed to unseat the Unionist mayor he was pitted against, but he continued his close association with Paisley and was active with him in the tricolour riots campaign a few weeks later. He also joined the B Specials.

In 1965 Doherty offered to put his experience in the printing trade at the service of his master. He formulated a scheme, which Paisley approved, for procuring second-hand type and a flat-bed press for the production first of pamphlets and later of a regular newspaper. The Puritan Printing Company opened shop in a grubby basement in Ravenhill Road, opposite Paisley's church, with Paisley and Doherty as directors. Six months later, in May 1966, it turned out the first edition of the fortnightly *Protestant Telegraph*.

Doherty seems to have been a devoted and unquestioning admirer of 'the Big Man'. Augustus ('Gusty') Spence was an altogether harder character. The Spences were a well-known clan on the lower Shankill. Gusty's elder brother, William, had been prominent in Unionist Party politics and had been election agent to James Kilfedder in West Belfast.

Gusty's earliest prominence was in 1959 when he was still a serving soldier in the British army and had just completed a spell in Cyprus as a military policeman. When Gerry Fitt, then an up-and-coming Republican Labour councillor on Belfast corporation, attacked British troops as 'murdering thugs', Spence organised a 'loyalist' march on the City Hall and persuaded Paisley to address a rally on the steps. When Spence completed his army service and took a job at Harland and Wolff, he became prominent in Ulster Protestant Action. Spence was a 'stager', a difficult and dangerous job involving the construction of scaffolding within which new ships take shape. 'Stagers' were tough. They were also exclusively protestant and the vanguard of 'loyalist' extremism in the shipyards.

It was men like Paisley, Doherty and Spence who, in one way or another, came to the fore at times of tension in Northern Ireland. The first weeks of 1966 were just such a time, with rumours of an IRA revival, the impending celebrations of 1916 and the bitter squabbling over the refusal of Belfast corporation to call their new bridge after the revered Carson.

When Carson's son, Edward, made an unaccustomed intrusion into Ulster politics by publicly complaining that his father had been 'treated with scant veneration by successive governments', Paisley took him up and wheeled him around the province in a temperature-raising, whistle-stop tour. Paisley made it known that he was considering forming a new organisation which would unite all 'true loyalists' within a Carson-Paisley partnership, and on 1 March, at a rally in Lisburn, Carson proved that he could match the violence of his mentor's rhetoric. Of the Governor, Lord Erskine, who had led the successful campaign to name the bridge after the Queen, Carson declared: 'He must go. There are two ways in which he could be relieved. I am going to continue gunning for this man.'

And on the very day of the Lisburn rally, Belfast newspaper offices received anonymous telephone calls 'threatening that any attempt by the IRA to use force against the RUC will be met by force on the basis of "a life for a life" '. The *Belfast Newsletter* reported: 'The Northern Ireland Government is enquiring into reports that the UVF is being re-formed in county Tyrone to oppose IRA and Republican plans to hold parades at Easter.'

Ulster was tumbling headlong into its own history. And no one in the province, protestant or catholic, was in any doubt as to what was implied in a threat to revive the Ulster Volunteer Force.

4 PAISLEY, SPENCE AND THE UVF

Ulster's own tormented politics were thrown into confusion when Harold Wilson sprang a Westminster general election for 31 March. Paisley's immediate response was to announce that he would field four Protestant Unionist candidates, including Edward Carson in his father's old seat of North Belfast. But just before nominations closed, the Paisleyites suddenly pulled out. With all his growing popularity in the protestant ghettos, and despite his string of twenty Free Presbyterian churches, Paisley was forced to face up to the fact that he did not command an adequate electoral machine. 'Protestant Unionism' was a label only: there were no local Protestant Unionist associations, no members, no finances. This had to be remedied before a realistic challenge could be made to official Unionism.

The driving force behind the construction of a political vehicle for Paisleyite politics was Noel Doherty. Having got the Puritan Printing Company off the ground, and with the first issue of the *Protestant Telegraph* already in preparation, Doherty was about to father his most important brainchild: the Ulster Constitution Defence Committee.

Early in April, within a few days of Wilson's consolidating victory – which did nothing to ease the insecurity of the 'loyalist' ultras – Paisley called a meeting of friends at his home in Beersbridge Road, Belfast, to discuss Doherty's proposal. That night saw the formation of a '12-man united society of protestant patriots pledged by all lawful methods to uphold and maintain the constitution of Northern Ireland'. Paisley was appointed chairman and Doherty secretary. The committee was familiarly known as 'the twelve disciples'.

But Doherty was also engaged in freelance activities of his own. His position as a trusted lieutenant of Paisley had given him contacts all over Ulster, and at least two months before the UCDC was formed he had begun to organise some of these contacts into a network of 'Ulster Protestant Volunteer Corps'. The Lisburn rally addressed by Edward Carson and Paisley on 1 March was organised by one such corps which had adopted the motto of the old UVF, 'For God and Ulster'. It may well have been Doherty's UPV corps which gave rise to the report that the government was investigating rumours that the UVF was being re-formed. The RUC Special Branch also began investigations into an outbreak of petrol-bomb attacks on catholic schools and bars.

Then on 20 March a Belfast woman who had written to the press complaining about the violence of Carson's Lisburn speech received the following anonymous letter:

Dear Madam,
As loyal Ulster Protestants we feel it our duty to take this matter into our hands. As we can see from your letter in the *Belfast Telegraph*, you are not an Ulster Protestant or even a Protestant of any sort because a Protestant believes in standing on the grounds of our forefathers and the Reformers and willing to shed our blood for the glorious cause of the Gospel. Let us as Protestants warn you if you insult the name of Lord Carson or any loyal man who stands for the true sort of Protestantism, because we are in full force against this matter and will see at all cost that you will be silent in the days to come unless there is an apology in the *Belfast Telegraph*. This is a warning letter – only we thought it better as you are a woman to give you time to repent.

The letter was signed 'UVF Secretary'. Whether it came from one of the Volunteer corps formed by Doherty is impossible to say. What we do know is that by this time a body calling itself the UVF had been formed on

35

the lower Shankill. And, as we shall see later, Doherty had connections with it.

The leading spirit of Shankill UVF was thirty-three-year-old Gusty Spence. What little we know of the earliest actions of this body is gleaned from police statements and depositions made by men who were subsequently charged and convicted of criminal offences. These statements indicate that, like Doherty's Volunteer corps, Spence's organisation was formed in March. Its first recorded action was on the night of 16 April when two members of the group drove past the Shankill home of the right-wing Unionist MP for Woodvale, John McQuade, and fired two bullets through his door in a mock IRA attack.

Next day saw the public debut of the Paisley-Doherty UCDC organisation in a parade from Shankill Road to the Ulster Hall. The procession stopped off briefly at the cenotaph to lay a wreath 'in memory of the members of the UVF, RUC and other civilian population who died in defence of the Ulster constitution at the hands of British forces during and since the 1916 Rising'. Inside the Ulster Hall, Paisley thundered that 'the principles for which our forefathers had fought and died, and the principles which brought the UVF into existence, had been defied and defiled'. That was clearly a reference to the old UVF. But then, according to an RUC Special Branch report of the meeting, he 'thanked all those who had come along and marched that day, and specially mentioned the UVF by name'.

As it happens, we know that both Spence's and Doherty's Volunteers were on that march. As it passed down the Shankill Road it passed McDowell's Bar. Two men, William Blakely and Leslie Porter, left Gusty Spence at the bar and joined the parade, teaming up with a group of Shankill UVF members including Hugh McClean, Desmond Reid and George Bigger. These five men skipped Paisley's Ulster Hall rally and spent the evening in a nearby pub. After the rally they rejoined the parade for its return to the Shankill, but Porter, Bigger and Blakely broke away when they reached Crimea Street and made their way towards Crumlin Road which separates the protestant Shankill from catholic Ardoyne. They were armed, Porter with a loaded Smith and Wesson revolver, Blakely with a Colt automatic. Shots were fired through the window of a shop they believed (wrongly) to be owned by a catholic, and the trio then made a hasty retreat. Two days later McClean told Porter he had been 'accepted as a member of the UVF, Shankill Division'. Porter was later sworn in by Spence at a meeting in a house in Belgrave Street and handed his gun over for Spence's safe-keeping.

Another chain of events also began at Paisley's UCDC demonstration. Among those who joined the parade was a member of Armagh Free Presbyterian Church named James Murdoch, a distributor of religious tracts. At the Ulster Hall he met Noel Doherty. Doherty told him about the Volunteer corps he was forming and said he would like to get one going in Loughgall, where Murdoch lived. Murdoch agreed to call a meeting of potential members at his house the following Thursday, 21 April.

On the appointed evening, Paisley drove Doherty to Loughgall and dropped him at Murdoch's house. Paisley did not attend the meeting himself, but drove on to a service in Armagh. The discussion for the first half of the meeting, according to Murdoch, was 'mainly about the ecumenical movement'. Later it turned to 'gelignite and guns'. A quarryman named Jim Marshall said he could get hold of explosives. The general trend of the conversation was that, in the event of any police or members of the Ulster Special Constabulary being shot, 'reprisals might be taken against the IRA'. At about 11 o'clock Paisley called, joined them for a cup of tea and drove Doherty back to Belfast. Doherty later emphasised that Paisley knew nothing of what was discussed. Paisley was also at pains to make this clear. But the meeting was called and chaired by the secretary of the Ulster Constitution Defence Committee, of which Paisley was chairman. The activities discussed suggest that the UPV and the UVF were not much differentiated in Doherty's mind, or in the minds of some of Paisley's church members.

On the day after the Loughgall meeting, the UCDC met and decided in principle to start organising local branches. On 2 May it was decided that these branches would take the form of 'Ulster Protestant Volunteer Divisions'. How the decision was arrived at is not clear. Possibly Doherty persuaded his UCDC colleagues to take under their wing the UPV corps he had already formed. Possibly the initiative came from Paisley, seeking a way of bringing a proliferation of 'loyalist' groups under his personal control. However that may be, after 2 May Doherty's Volunteer corps were UPV 'divisions' of the UCDC, bound by a constitution and rules which made strenuous and significant efforts to dissociate the movement from illegal violence. The rules provided that 'any member associated with, or giving support to, any subversive or lawless activities whatsoever shall be expelled from the body. The chairman of the UCDC has vested in him full authority to act in all such cases'. And to meet the criticism that the word 'divisions' had a military flavour, it was stated that the Volunteers took their name 'from the Parliamentary Division in which they are situated'.

The UCDC was defined as the 'governing body' and 'executive' of the UPV. Only 'born protestants' were eligible for membership: anyone who had ever been a Roman Catholic was automatically excluded. So were members of the RUC but not, significantly, the Special Constabulary. Although provision was made for 'representative meetings' to which each UPV division was entitled to send one voting delegate, the executive itself was self-appointed and self-perpetuating. Finally, the rules provided, in a point of crucial significance, that 'When the authorities act contrary to the Constitution the body will take *whatever steps it thinks fit* to expose such unconstitutional acts.'

At the best of times, the sponsorship of bodies calling themselves Volunteer divisions was likely to cause alarm in the catholic community. And these were not the best of times. There were continuing rumours of clandestine activity in the name of the UVF. Questions were asked in Stormont about 'an organisation of law-breakers at Loughgall' where 'members of an illegal armed organisation of Unionist extremists' were said to be 'actively drilling'. The petrol-bomb attacks on catholic premises in March were followed by five more in April and the first week of May. Confusion was inevitable, and Labour MP Tom Boyd expressed the thoughts of many when he said of the UCDC and its branches: 'Another private army is beginning to develop in our community.'

Paisley did little in these early weeks to discourage direct association of the UPV divisions with the name of the old UVF. On 10 May at a UPV recruiting meeting in Lisburn Orange Hall he 'proclaimed that the new Volunteers would be guided by the UVF motto "For God and Ulster" '. He was to tell the Scarman tribunal five years later that the name 'Ulster Protestant Volunteer divisions' was chosen 'because I think it had a historic connection with the foundation of this State, with Carson's Ulster Volunteer Force'.

Meanwhile the spate of petrol-bombing of catholic premises accelerated. On 7 May a bomb was tossed from a passing car towards the windows of a catholic-owned bar in Upper Charleville Street. It missed, and went through the window of the adjoining terraced house. In the blaze that followed, the occupant, an elderly protestant named Mrs Martha Gould, was burned to death. The attack subsequently proved to be the work of the Shankill UVF, and the man who threw the petrol-bomb was jailed on a firearms charge. Awarding Mrs Gould's widower

39

compensation from public funds some months later, a Belfast judge declared the bombing to be the work of 'the Ulster Protestant Volunteer Force', described as 'a seditious combination or unlawful association' whose activities were 'directed to asserting and maintaining the protestant ascendancy in areas of the city where there was a predominantly protestant majority of the local population'. It sought to effect this, said the judge, 'by overt acts of annoyance and even terrorism'.

On 21 May the Belfast newspapers received a message, the first of many in the next six years, from 'Captain William Johnston, chief-in-staff of the UVF':

From this day on we declare war against the IRA and its splinter groups. Known IRA men will be executed mercilessly and without hesitation. Less extreme measures will be taken against anyone sheltering or helping them, but if they persist in giving them aid then more extreme methods will be adopted. Property will not be exempted in any action taken. We will not tolerate any interference from any source and we solemnly warn the authorities to make no more speeches of appeasement. We are heavily armed Protestants dedicated to this cause.

On 26 May the Shankill UVF started holding regular Thursday night meetings in a back room of the Standard Bar. The barman understood the meetings were arranged by a 'social organisation', and Spence – who did not publicly admit his involvement with the UVF until six years later – claimed that they were merely planning meetings for the Shankill's celebrations of the Twelfth of July. But other participants have made it clear that less innocent matters were also discussed.

At the 26 May meeting it was decided to eliminate Leo Martin, a prominent Republican associated with the Belfast brigade of the IRA. Four men arranged to do the job the following evening. They were driving through the Clonard in a fruitless search for Martin when they passed a stranger making his tipsy way home after an evening's drinking. He was happily singing to himself, running through a repertoire of popular Republican songs. They decided he was an IRA man. He was shot and left to crawl to the door of his home a few yards down the road. An anonymous phone call to the *Belfast Telegraph* claimed UVF responsibility for the 'execution' and when the man, John Scullion, died on 11 June, the police investigation became a murder hunt.

On the weekend after Scullion's murder another member of Shankill UVF, Robert Williamson, led an armed hold-up at McMahon's off-licence in Tennent Street. Shortly after closing time on Saturday 4 June the proprietor, James McMahon, opened the door to find Williamson and another man on the doorstep. Williamson had a Colt .45 revolver in his hand. McMahon slammed the door and the two raiders fled. 'I wanted to get money for the UVF. I got the revolver from the pool of arms of the UVF,' said Williamson later.

There were, then, two distinct groups of 'Volunteers' active in Ulster, each laying claim to the mantle of the old UVF. One was the UPV body affiliated to the UCDC, of which Paisley was chairman and Doherty secretary. Its constitution specifically condemned 'subversive or lawless activities'; but, as we have seen, the inaugural meeting of at least one 'division', Loughgall, had discussed 'gelignite and guns' and 'reprisals against the IRA'. The other body was Spence's UVF, which was already taking the law into its own hands.

Was there any connection between the two groups, beyond the known participation of Spence's UVF in Paisley's UCDC parade on 17 April?

There was. And the link was Noel Doherty.

Soon after the Loughgall meeting, Desmond Reid and George Bigger of Shankill UVF called at Doherty's Belfast home and asked if he could help them obtain gelignite to blow up 'IRA monuments'. On 21 May (which was also the day of Captain William Johnston's UVF communiqué to the *Belfast Telegraph*) Doherty took Bigger to Loughgall. They delivered some UCDC pamphlets to Murdoch's house and Murdoch introduced them to Jim Marshall, the quarryman who had talked of gelignite at the earlier meeting. Marshall agreed to help and a week later, on 28 May, Reid and Bigger collected from his home twenty-seven sticks of gelignite, six detonators and a length of wire. The explosives were removed to Bigger's house in Glengormley, then hidden in a milk churn in a shed behind a disused farmhouse. A further meeting was held in Bigger's house a day or two later, when Doherty was shown sticks of gelignite and a gun. The talk was of obtaining more arms and killing IRA leaders. Doherty, according to his own account much later, began to feel that 'things were going too far. As I was a member of the Ulster Special Constabulary, seeing firearms in the hands of men who could not handle them really frightened me.'

In view of later unsubstantiated rumours that the UVF was secretly arming Paisley's Ulster Protestant Volunteers, it is ironic to record that the reverse was true. Doherty, Paisley's right-hand man, was the intermediary through whom members of Loughgall UPV supplied gelignite to Shankill UVF.

Paisley himself was busy elsewhere. On 6 June the Presbyterian Church held its annual General Assembly in Fisherwick Place, Belfast, and Paisley, who saw the church's ecumenical and liberal trend as the spiritual rationale for O'Neill's political appeasement, planned to picket the meeting. The picket was preceded by a parade to Fisherwick Place, and the route ran through Cromac Square, one of the oldest catholic areas in Belfast.

A riot was inevitable. As the parade passed through the square, stones, bottles and scrap-iron rained down on the marchers, who hurried on, leaving an undermanned police force to cope as best it could with a worsening situation. Four policemen were badly injured. None of the marchers was hurt. 'When one thinks of over 600 people walking through such an onslaught unharmed,' commented Paisley later, 'one can only praise the Lord.' The policemen clearly didn't count, and from that incident dates the hostility of a significant section of the RUC towards Paisley. This hostility was sometimes publicly expressed, and Paisley was not slow to claim that he was the victim of trumped-up police plots.

Protected by the police through Cromac Square, the parade found itself barred from Fisherwick Place by a police cordon. Some marchers tried to break through and there was more violence. There were accusations of foul language from the Paisleyites, which Paisley put down, improbably, to 'Romanists mingling in our crowd'. Eventually he was arrested, along with two other Free Presbyterian ministers, a Protestant Unionist councillor and a lady member of his church who was soon, quite fortuitously, to provide further evidence that, at least on the Shankill, the UVF and the UPV were one and the same organisation.

O'Neill took this failure of law and order so seriously that he sent Home Affairs Minister Brian McConnell to apologise to the presbyterians. Paisley promised in return that 'in the very near future we will take action to prove to every citizen of this country that, as Protestants, we are as determined as the gun-runners of Larne not to bow to tyranny from any source.'

Official Unionism now took steps to dissociate itself altogether from that part of its own past which persisted in lingering on as Paisleyism. The Orange Order denounced 'extremism', the Presbyterian Church went to some pains to prove that Free Presbyterianism was wholly unconnected with historical presbyterianism. The *Belfast Telegraph* declared that Paisley's organisations 'represent a defiance of lawful authority no less serious in essence than that of the IRA,' and urged Northern Ireland to 'protect

43

itself against an attempt to subvert it by a new and vicious form of terrorism'. Unionist Party leaders fell over themselves to get their protestations on record. To Roy Bradford, Paisley was 'this latter-day Luther of the lumpenproletariat' whose preaching was 'the very rabies of religion'. Terence O'Neill commented that 'if a fascist movement were allowed to rule the roost in Ulster then our constitution might indeed be in danger'. And he went on:

To those of us who remember the 'thirties the pattern is horribly familiar. The contempt for established authority; the crude and unthinking intolerance; the emphasis upon monster processions and rallies; the appeal to a perverted form of patriotism; each and every one of these things has its parallel in the rise of the Nazis to power. A minority movement was able, in the end, to work its will simply because most people were too apathetic or too intimidated to speak out. History must not be allowed to repeat itself in this small corner of the Commonwealth.

But more insulting to some of Paisley's supporters, perhaps because phrased in language they could not fail to understand, was Nat Minford's description of the UCDC chairman as a 'big windbag' and a 'bloated bullfrog'. Minford promptly received two anonymous letters. One said: 'Shut your big mouth Minford or we will get you one night on a dark lane.' The other said: 'Minford, we have a personal date and the bullet is ready for it.' His wife also received an anonymous phone call: 'Tell Minford to shut his mouth or we will put a bullet between his eyes and shut his mouth permanently.'

Then on 9 June Minford received a telegram:

THE OFFICERS AND MEMBERS OF THE 1ST SHANKILL DIVISION UVF WILL NOT TOLERATE YOUR LIES AND DUPLICITY NO LONGER STOP HUNDRED PER CENT BEHIND IAN PAISLEY.

The telegram too was anonymous. But on the reverse side the post office counter clerk who had taken it had filled in the sender's name and address: '1st Shankill UVF, 48 Geoffrey Street, Belfast'.

At no. 48 lived Mrs 'Mina' Browne, a middle-aged part-time cleaner and attender at Paisley's church. She was well-known on the Shankill as a 'loyalist' militant and a member of Ulster Protestant Action. In 1963 she won some notoriety by leading what became known as the 'Mrs Mopps march' against a corporation decision to include catholics on the roll of school cleaners. On 6 June 1966 she was one of the six people arrested with Paisley at the Presbyterian General Assembly disturbances.

Stormont appointed a four-man committee to investigate the origin of the telegram and decide whether it constituted intimidation of an MP, and therefore a breach of parliamentary privilege. One of the members was Desmond Boal, the barrister who had defended Paisley on the Donald Soper charge in 1959 and had since been elected, with Paisley's support, as Unionist MP for Shankill. Boal was at one and the same time Paisley's legal advisor and assistant to the Attorney-General. To compound his problem, he now found himself on a committee investigating the behaviour of an associate of Paisley's. A few days later he resigned his position with the Attorney-General and also quarrelled with the chairman of the investigating committee, after which the three remaining members were left alone to make what they could of the strange case of Mrs Mina Browne.

Mrs Browne told the committee that she was 'an organiser for the organisation called the Ulster Protestant Volunteers'. She belonged to the 1st Shankill Division UPV and had met Paisley when he was guest speaker at a meeting of 'the group'. She had acted on her own initiative, she said, in sending the telegram, which was only intended as a warning that the group would put up a candidate against him at the next election. She had signed it '1st Shankill UVF,' she said, 'to make it sound more important'. Then she added, significantly, 'It should not have been UVF, it should have been Ulster Protestant Volunteers.'

In Mrs Browne's mind, at least, the two were much the same.

The committee pressed her on whether she really had acted alone. Evidence was given by the post office clerk that, when handing in the telegram, Mrs Browne had been accompanied by a man. A *Belfast Telegraph* reporter said that Mrs Browne had called at the paper's offices to give them a copy of the telegram, and had been accompanied by a man who gave his name and address as 'George Johnston, 55 Ashley Avenue'. No such person could be found. Mrs Browne first said that there was no man with her, then said she didn't want to involve him, then said she didn't know his name. She finally admitted that she had first met him three months earlier at a Paisley meeting in the Ulster Hall, 'through the organisation'. The committee concluded that her answers were 'carefully rehearsed', 'evasive' and 'untruthful'. It 'did not accept her evidence that she was solely responsible' for the telegram. But in the event, no action was taken against her or against 1st Shankill Division UPV–UVF.

Clearly Mrs Browne was shielding someone, presumably someone of importance since her prevarications jeopardised her own defence. In the light of later events there was speculation that the man with her, calling himself 'Johnston', was Gusty Spence. He wasn't. He was Noel Doherty. Months later, when the RUC Special Branch were questioning him on other matters, Doherty made a statement in which he said: 'During this time [June], Mrs Browne of Geoffrey Street requested that I word a telegram on behalf of her branch to send to Mr Minford, which I did: "The officers and members of the 1st Shankill UPV will not tolerate your duplicity and lies against loyalists any longer".'

Little wonder, then, that Mrs Browne, as a loyal Paisleyite, went to some lengths to cover up for the

46

founder and first secretary of the UCDC, who acted now in the name of the UPV, now in that of the UVF.

After the Minford telegram incident, Paisley was quick to tell the press that 'it was incorrect to describe the Ulster Volunteer divisions as the UVF'. But the prevailing confusion of names and initials was not made any clearer when Paisley told an Ulster Hall rally on 16 June: 'Let me tell you this, friends, there are many ex-servicemen at this meeting. They are the defenders of the flag of Ulster. I have a resolution here from some of them, the ex-servicemen of both world wars, now comprising four divisions of the UVF: "We are solidly behind Rev. Paisley . . . and we give him our entire support".'

On 23 June Labour MP Tom Boyd pressed O'Neill to use the Special Powers Act to ban 'the organisations which he described as fascist in character'. O'Neill replied that there was no indication that the organisations referred to were 'contemplating physical violence'. That night Captain and Mrs O'Neill flew to Paris to observe the fiftieth anniversary of the wiping out of the old UVF on the Somme. And as they left Belfast, Spence's Shankill UVF held its weekly meeting in the Standard Bar and decided on 'targets' for the coming weekend.

5 MURDER IN MALVERN STREET

Belfast begins its celebrations of the Twelfth early. On Saturday 25 June, Prince Albert Temperance Loyal Orange Lodge No. 1892 opened the marching season with a parade down the Shankill Road. It was led by one of the lodge's most distinguished members, the local MP John McQuade, whose house, it will be remembered, had been shot up two months earlier in a mock-IRA raid by the Shankill UVF. Two UVF members paraded with McQuade on 25 June. One was Robert Williamson, the other Gusty Spence, who was also a member of the Apprentice Boys and the Royal Black Preceptory.

When the parade of the Temperance Lodge ended, Spence and Williamson called at the Four-Step Inn for some refreshment. From there they moved on to the Rex Bar and from there to the Standard Bar, where they held their weekly Shankill UVF meetings. There they met up with Hugh McClean, Leslie Porter, Desmond Reid, a cousin of Spence's named Henry Hayes, and James 'Rocky' Burns. Burns was important to them. A forty-six-year-old labourer, he had served a prison sentence during the war. There he had come to know a number of IRA internees whose names and addresses were now made available to the UVF.

After a few rounds of drinks, they all repaired to a back room and began a meeting. Reid and Porter were sent to meet a man named Robert Winters, of Armagh, who had been present at the meeting in Loughgall on 21 April when gelignite was discussed. Winters duly arrived, believing, he claimed later, that he was attending 'a UCDC meeting'. Then Reid was sent out again, this time to collect the gelignite hidden in a milk churn earlier that month.

According to the full account given by Hugh McClean in a number of subsequent statements to the police, Spence chaired the meeting and did most of the talking. Spence named as the 'target for the night' Leo Martin, whom the UVF had tried to find a month earlier on the night John Scullion was killed instead. Rocky Burns supplied the information that Martin lived in Baden-Powell Street but he didn't know the number, so Porter was sent to find out. When he returned, Burns and McClean were sent out with him. Spence checked that McClean was carrying his gun. 'Burns and I were told we were to shoot Martin,' McClean said in his statements.

They drove to Baden-Powell Street and got out of the car. According to McClean, 'Burns and I arranged that we would knock on Martin's door and if he answered the door we would shoot him.' But Martin was out. Burns decided to break in through a window and start a fire. They then returned to the Standard Bar and reported back to Spence. They had a few more drinks and moved on to the home of Spence's sister, Mrs Cassie Curry, in Belgrave Street. 'We all sat down and talked about arms,' said McClean. 'Spence did most of the talking. He talked mostly of getting more arms to arm the Volunteers.'

At about ten o'clock they left for another round of drinks at the Malvern Arms, a bar known for keeping late hours. 'When we were in the bar about an hour,' McClean's account continued, 'four lads came into the bar and went to drink at the counter.' They were Andrew Kelly, Liam Doyle, Richard Leppington and eighteen-year-old Peter Ward, all barmen at the International Hotel, Belfast. All four were from the south and spoke with southern accents.

The conversation came up about the religion of these fellows. Spence asked the company if they would be catholics . . . Spence then went up to the bar beside the four lads to buy a drink. When he returned to our table he said: 'I have been listening to their conversation and they are four IRA men'. We had some more drinks . . . Spence said: 'These are IRA men, they will have to go.'

Shortly after midnight, according to McClean's evidence, McClean, Spence and Williamson left the bar with an unnamed fourth man and took up positions in the street outside. At about 1.45 the four barmen came out by the side door. Ward was shot dead and Kelly and Doyle were seriously wounded. Ironically, Ward was gunned down under a wall slogan reading 'Up the UVF'. The gunmen fled to Spence's sister's house. 'Spence produced a sack,' said McClean, 'and we all put our guns into it and it was left on the floor. Somebody produced a bottle of porter and I drank it. Spence said: "That's the job done", or words to that effect.'

The UVF execution squad and the four catholic visitors were not the only late drinkers in the Malvern Arms that night. A party of off-duty RUC men were in a back room. Within hours arrests were made and statements taken. On the morning of 28 June Spence, Williamson and McClean were charged with the capital crime of murder in furtherance of a seditious conspiracy in that they 'on divers dates between March 1 and June 27 1966 conspired together, and with other persons unknown, to incite illwill among the different classes and creeds of the Queen's subjects, to create a public disturbance and disorder and to injure and murder persons who might be opposed to their opinions'. Porter and Reid were charged with possessing explosive substances with intent to endanger life and property, and Blakely, Bigger and Burns were arrested on firearms charges. Spence was also charged with the murder of John Scullion.

Spence and McClean were to make a number of complaints at their treatment under interrogation by the police. Spence's arrest was later described by his friend John McKeague in *Loyalist News*:

He asked for a solicitor and was laughed at, he asked for food and was sneered at, he asked to see the officer in charge of the station and was told he had 'no chance'. He was told the phones were out of order when he requested the use of it. Twenty-four detectives working in relays of four grilled and questioned him, threatening him, so as to make a statement, for over 18 hours. He refused to make any statement, he was struck on repeated occasions and we have the names of the police officers who used the brutality.

The police charged that Spence said in arrest: 'So this is what you get for being a protestant!' McClean, pressed to tell how he had come to join the UVF, was said by the police to have replied: 'I was asked did I agree with Paisley, and was I prepared to follow him. I said that I was.' After being charged, he allegedly said: 'I am terribly sorry I ever heard tell of that man Paisley or decided to follow him. I am definitely ashamed of myself to be in such a position.'

Within hours of the murder, protestant churchmen hurried to condemn it. One of the first public pronouncements came from Ian Paisley. He told the *Belfast News-letter*:

Like everyone else I deplore and condemn this killing, as all right-thinking people must. Incitement, direct or indirect, must be treated with the full rigour of the law. Under the Special Powers Act the government has the full authority to act and has failed to do so. If it continues to abdicate its responsibilities then the British government must act immediately in its place.

In the light of the ambiguity of his own relationship with the UVF up to that point, this was an extraordinary statement. Whether or not he recognised or cared to admit it, the UVF was largely a product of his own rhetoric and some of his closest associates were UVF men. Now Paisley had the gall to claim that O'Neill was to blame for what had happened by not banning the UVF earlier. Paisley was already beginning to prove himself a deft politician, but he failed to deflect a storm of recrimination against himself and his organisations.

As we have seen, on the weekend of the murder O'Neill was in France attending a ceremony commemorating the men of the old UVF. On the Monday night he was summoned back to Belfast where, in the early hours of Tuesday, he was briefed in an emergency cabinet meeting. Later that day he told Stormont:

Information which has come to hand in the last few days makes it clear that the safety of law-abiding citizens is threatened by a very dangerous conspiracy prepared at any time to use murder as a weapon . . . The Minister of Home Affairs has this morning made regulations under the Civil Authorities (Special Powers) Act (N.I.) 1932 to declare an organisation which has misappropriated the title 'UVF' an unlawful organisation . . . This organisation now takes its proper place alongside the IRA in the schedule of illegal bodies.

The *Belfast Telegraph* reported 'a widespread impression . . . after the Premier's speech . . . that the Rev. Ian Paisley's movement was now banned'. But Paisley told a meeting at Holywood, county Down, on the night of the ban: 'The Ulster Constitution Defence Committee has absolutely no association with the UVF. I don't know what the UVF is or who its leaders are, or what its intentions are.'

Of McClean's reference to himself, Paisley said: 'This is to try to tie me up with this atrocious murder. I don't know Mr McClean. He is not a Free Presbyterian . . . Mr McClean never was a member of the UCDC, never was a member of the UPV divisions and he has never been associated with me at all.' He added: 'We are not fascists, we are Protestants. We want to tell Captain O'Neill that the men who formed our divisions are men who fought for the Flag against fascism, and please God they will do it again if need be . . . This incident that has happened is deplorable, but it is not as deplorable as those in which policemen like Norman Anderson were brutally butchered by the IRA [in the 1950s border campaign].'

The *Protestant Telegraph* added more denials: 'Mr Paisley has never advocated violence, has never been associated with the UVF and has always opposed the hell-soaked liquor traffic which constituted the background to this murder.'

O'Neill poured scorn on all these efforts by Paisley to dissociate himself from the UVF: 'He is no doubt anxious to wash his hands of it now, but the record clearly shows that he has hitherto received and welcomed their support.' O'Neill quoted 'verbatim police reports' of the speeches made by Paisley at his Ulster Hall rallies on 17 April and 16 June when, on the first occasion, he was said to have 'thanked all those who had marched that day and specifically mentioned the UVF by name,' and on the second, read a resolution of support from 'ex-service-men of both world wars, now comprising four divisions of the UVF'. O'Neill concluded that 'Members will be able to judge for themselves the extent to which Mr Paisley can properly claim ignorance of the activities of the UVF'.

Paisley has made inconsistent attempts to explain away the reports quoted by O'Neill. When the two quotations were put to him at the Scarman hearings five years later, he flatly denied having made the statements attributed to him. On other occasions he has claimed that he was referring to veterans of Carson's UVF. But it would be surprising if such a body had marched unnoticed on 17 April, or if four divisions of veterans had attended the 16 June rally without attracting attention. In fact, the files of the *Belfast Newsletter* reveal that when he was originally questioned about O'Neill's accusations, Paisley in effect admitted that on at least one of the two occasions he *was* referring to the new UVF. The *Newsletter* of 30 June quotes him as complaining that O'Neill's reference to the 17 April meeting 'failed to state that it was in answer to a press query that I said we would welcome the members of the UVF just as we would welcome the members of the USC. Let it be pointed out also that when I mentioned the UVF there had been no accusations or insinuations made about its activities by Captain O'Neill'.

When banning the UVF, O'Neill also charged that 'a leading member of the UVF is also a prominent official of the so-called Ulster Constitution Defence Committee, of which Mr Paisley is the publicly acknowledged chairman'. Although O'Neill failed to name the man, probably to avoid prejudicing possible court proceedings, this was clearly a reference to Noel Doherty, who had been pulled in for questioning. Paisley flatly denied that any member of the UCDC was connected with the UVF, and so far as Doherty was concerned he had already taken steps to break the link. With the UCDC vice-chairman, James McConnell, he called at Doherty's home, took possession of the UCDC minute book and told Doherty he was summarily expelled from the movement he had helped found. His connections with the Puritan Printing Company and the *Protestant Telegraph* were also broken off. Doherty had got into trouble and his usefulness to the man he had served for just over ten years was suddenly at an end.

Amid enormous public interest, the preliminary hearings on the Malvern Street murder opened in Belfast before the Resident Magistrate, Mr Gerald Lynn, on 18 August. The purpose of such a hearing is to enable the magistrate to determine whether or not there is sufficient evidence to warrant a case going to trial. Spence, McClean and Williamson all pleaded not guilty to the capital charge of conspiracy to murder. The defence began with a denial by McClean's attorney, Mr Michael Nicholson, of McClean's 'alleged verbal statement' referring to Paisley. 'There was a flagrant breach of the Judges' Rules in the taking of these statements,' claimed Nicholson. But the magistrate declined to rule against McClean's four depositions. In the third of these, part of which I have already quoted, McClean described Spence as his 'immediate boss' in Shankill UVF, but said he thought he was taking orders from someone else. He described how the group had met the four catholic barmen, how Spence had decided they were IRA men who would 'have to go', and how he and Spence had participated in the shooting in Malvern Street.

Desmond Reid described his journey with Doherty to Armagh to obtain gelignite, and his participation in the meeting in the back room of the Standard Bar on the night of the murder. Asked whether this was a UVF meeting, he said he didn't listen to what was being said. But he had heard of the UVF and wanted to join it. He understood it was 'the same as the UCDC, which organises parades and one thing and another'.

On the fourth day Williamson made two statements, one corroborating McClean's account of the killing and the other describing the earlier raid on McMahon's Bar 'to get money for the UVF to buy arms'. On the fifth day Joseph Watson, proprietor of the Malvern Arms, gave evidence that Spence and his friends had been in the bar on the night of 25 June, that they had left just after half-past-midnight, and that the four victims of the shooting had left by a side door at about 1.45 a.m.

There then followed an extraordinary conflict of interpretation over the evidence offered by a ballistics expert, Dr Martin. The court had difficulty in deciding whether Dr Martin's evidence meant that three or four guns had been fired that night. McClean, it will be remembered, had insisted in his statement that a fourth man, whose name he said he didn't know, had taken part. If this was so, and if Dr Martin's evidence bore this out, then the prosecution was clearly one prisoner short. But the magistrate decided that only three guns had been used – a ruling that failed to stop widespread speculation on the identity of the mystery 'fourth man'. One popular theory on the Shankill was that he was later appointed UVF chief-of-staff after Spence's imprisonment. Another theory had it that he escaped prosecution by informing on Spence, and supporters of this version name the man and point out that he has since been the victim of several shooting attacks, described as UVF 'punitive actions'.

On the sixth day there was more drama. It was revealed in court that all three survivors of the shooting had failed to pick out Spence in an identification parade (though one subsequently claimed that he had recognised Spence but was too frightened to identify him). Then Spence himself gave evidence. He denied that he was a member of the UVF, and said he had spent the crucial period from 12.15 a.m. to 2 a.m. at his sister's house in Belgrave Street, not at the Malvern Arms.

Next day, 26 August, McClean and Williamson were returned for trial by jury. But the magistrate decided that there was no case against Spence. It took the intervention of the Attorney-General, overruling the magistrate, to get Spence before a jury – a procedure which, although by no means without precedent, was later cited as evidence of a 'political conspiracy' against the UVF leader. But the charge of murdering Scullion was dropped, and Spence was finally tried only for the Ward killing.

The trial proper began on 6 October before Lord Chief Justice McDermott and again the statements of McClean and Williamson formed the basis of the prosecution's case. Again McClean's counsel claimed that his statements were taken in circumstances which violated Judges' Rules: 'Anything said was the result of threats of physical violence and he was in so exhausted a state that he did not know what he was doing.' But Lord McDermott dismissed this claim and found that the statements had been taken voluntarily. Had his decision gone the other way, the outcome of the entire case might have been very different.

Spence claimed that at the meeting in the Standard Bar, before they moved on to the Malvern Arms, the group were discussing nothing more sinister than the erection of Orange street decorations in Lower Shankill in preparation for the Twelfth. He agreed that he had marched with the Prince Albert Temperance Lodge that day and had subsequently gone from the Four-Step Inn to the Rex Bar to the Standard Bar and to the Malvern Arms with Williamson and his cousin, Henry Hayes. McClean also gave evidence that Hayes had been in the Malvern Arms party. Spence claimed that, having left the bar at 12.15 a.m., about an hour-and-a-half before the shooting happened, he went straight to his sister's house and did not come out again. The jury were invited to conclude that, even if McClean and Williamson were convicted by their own statements, there was reasonable doubt that Spence was with them at the moment of the shooting.

So far the only direct evidence of Spence's participation in the shooting was the clear statement of his co-accused, McClean, and a less clear statement by his other co-accused, Williamson. But now the Crown wheeled on its star witness, Desmond Reid. Reid, it will be remembered, had left the meeting early to collect the Loughgall gelignite. In the round-up that followed the shooting the police had found the gelignite at his home and charged him and Leslie Porter with possessing explosive substances with intent to endanger life and damage property. But the charge against Reid was dropped when it was arranged for him to give evidence against Spence. The substance of his statement was that he had returned with the gelignite to Spence's sister's house. Then, 'some time after 1.30 a.m., Spence, McClean, Williamson and another chap came to the house and went into the scullery. I heard someone say "That was not a bad job". I didn't know who'.

That was enough for the jury. On 14 October they returned a verdict of murder against Spence, McClean and

57

Williamson. The three were found not guilty of the charge of conspiracy to murder, which still carried the death sentence. Lord McDermott sentenced them each to life imprisonment, recommending a minimum term of twenty years.

Four days later McDermott sent Noel Doherty down for two years jail on an explosives charge. Passing sentence, the judge told him: 'You have shown yourself in the character of an unstable man running from one enthusiasm to the other, no doubt under the pressure of other people's eloquence and the enthusiasm of the moment, to carry out your political ends.'

Jim Marshall, who supplied the gelignite, was fined £200. James Murdoch, in whose home the discussion of explosions had taken place, was found not guilty. Leslie Porter and Rocky Burns were convicted of firearms offences, Burns getting nine years. Porter volunteered the information: 'Spence is the Colonel of the Shankill Division so far as I know and his official name is Colonel William Johnston.'

Spence's appeal was turned down, as was a later petition for his release or retrial, organised by the UCDC. On both occasions it was stressed that Spence had been convicted on the evidence of his co-accused and that of an associate who had turned Queen's evidence. It was argued that such evidence would have been too slim to secure a conviction in an English court. Spence has continued to press, from Crumlin Road jail, for a retrial or a review of his case.

But if there is admitted to be a shadow of doubt as to whether his finger was on the trigger of one of the guns that killed Peter Ward, there is none about his leading role in the organisation which was proscribed for that crime. And for many of the lumpen elements who made up the UVF there was no essential conflict between 'the constitution' and protestant violence. 'The constitution' on the lips of Ulster 'loyalists' means not the mundane

58

law of the land but the higher law of protestant supremacy and ascendancy. From the Peep o' Day Boys to the UVF, protestant violence has been defended as 'constitutional' on the ground that, unlike the violence of the IRA, it seeks to uphold the protestant state by law established. The men of the UVF, new and old, knew that their actions were 'illegal', but they would have vehemently denied that they were 'unconstitutional'. As, in extremes, they were prepared to fight Britain to stay British, so they were prepared to break the law in order to defend it. Hence Doherty's ability to combine his office in the UCDC, pledged to act within the law, with illegal activity for the UVF. Hence Spence's disillusionment on arrest: 'So this is what you get for being a protestant!' Hence, too, the bizarre custom that has developed whereby the Prince Albert Temperance Orange Lodge, respectful of the law as it would certainly claim to be, stops at the gates of Crumlin Road jail on its annual Twelfth parade, and devotes a minute's silent homage to its two members inside, men convicted of murder – but in a protestant cause.

The UVF men were not the only protestant martyrs. On 19 July Paisley himself went to jail for three months after refusing to sign a pledge of good behaviour after the Presbyterian General Assembly riot. There were violent protests outside the jail and police used batons and water cannons to disperse protestant demonstrators who vented their fury by smashing shop windows and looting the displays. A Free Presbyterian parade to the City Hall, planned for the weekend after the sentences began, was confined by police to the Shankill Road area, and the RUC again used batons and water cannons when some marchers forced their way through the cordon and smashed more shop windows in the city centre. On 26 July the Minister of Home Affairs banned all processions and public meetings within a 15-mile radius of the City Hall, excepting only 'traditional' parades.

The riots were a reminder to Unionists of the violent alienation of their own traditional supporters. A group of Unionist backbenchers persuaded O'Neill to meet a UCDC deputation of Paisley's followers. Led by the Rev. Bert Cooke, acting Moderator of the Free Presbyterians in Paisley's absence, and the Rev. Brian Green, later a standard-bearer for the extreme-right National Front, a deputation saw the Prime Minister on 10 August. O'Neill told them there was nothing he could do to release the prisoners until they agreed to sign their bail bonds. Green issued a statement on behalf of the deputation:

The Prime Minister was told that thousands of people in Ulster and throughout the world considered that the imprisonment of the Rev. Ian Paisley and his colleagues was because of a political and ecclesiastical conspiracy. The Prime Minister denied this. The Premier was asked to make it clear to the British people, and in particular to the Westminster parliament, that the Free Presbyterian Church was not a group of gangsters, Fascists and Nazis and was not associated with subversive activities . . . The Prime Minister did not comment.

When Paisley was released on 19 October, his supporters celebrated by lighting fires all over protestant Belfast. The biggest, reported the *Belfast Newsletter* innocently, was in Malvern Street.

The Paisleyites had something to celebrate. A public opinion poll showed that 200,000 of Ulster's million protestants considered themselves potential Paisley supporters: this immediately after the General Assembly riots and at the height of the UVF affair. Paisley's growing 'extremism', in contrast to official Unionism's growing 'moderation', did nothing to repel working-class protestants. The classless coalition of Unionism began to break at the seams. That autumn, O'Neill faced the first of many challenges to his leadership and policies from Brian Faulkner and William Craig, men who knew a bandwagon when they saw it rolling and understood better than O'Neill that a Unionism which lost control of protestant workers was a Unionism on its death-bed.

Ulster's Volunteers – corps, divisions and forces – had put Northern Ireland on the road that finally led to the abandonment of Stormont and the collapse of Unionist power.

6 UNDERGROUND

After the cataclysmic year of 1966, 1967 was a year of comparative anti-climax. The UVF's leading spirits were in jail and little was heard of the movement. The Belfast newspapers received occasional communiqués from 'Capt. William Johnston, Shankill UVF', but these were treated by the RUC as crude attempts to suggest that, despite Spence's imprisonment, the real UVF leader was still at large. If he was, he chose to lie low. UVF members told me five years later that they made a deliberate decision in 1967 to 'go underground' and continue their activities. But that could be an empty boast. It is possible that the organisation simply fell apart and virtually ceased to exist for twelve months. Certainly members of the Spence family, many of whom were closely linked with Gusty politically, expended most of their energies that year in trying to whip up support for his retrial or release.

The May 1967 local elections in Belfast saw 'Protestant Unionist' representation on the corporation increase from two to three with the election of Mrs Paisley. The Free Presbyterians celebrated a more colourful victory when a group of them forced Jack Lynch to retreat to his official car under a rain of snowballs during a visit to Belfast for one of O'Neill's 'bridge building' sessions. The occasion was reported by Paisley's *Protestant Telegraph* with all the solemnity that might have been accorded the battle of the Boyne: 'When we read the Word of God we find that in the great victories of the Children of Israel in most cases God's servants used very simple means to rout their enemies . . . In 1967 God's servants used snowballs and God gave them the victory.'

Paisley's first priority was now the production of Noel Doherty's brainchild, the *Protestant Telegraph*. 'The Truth Shall Set You Free', it proclaimed below the masthead. Readers were assured of 'God's direct care and concern' for its contents. In twelve tabloid pages of unpolished prose it provided, fortnight by fortnight, a depressing record of protestant fear, prejudice, bigotry, bewilderment, frustration, puritan piety and occasional wit. It made no concession to good taste. The Church of England was 'a spiritual brothel, harbouring theological prostitutes and ecumenical pimps'. The Unionist Party was 'a political monstrosity, the product of ecumenism and Romanism'. But the most rabid invective was reserved for the Roman Catholic Church. 'Rome may paint her face and attire her hair like Jezebel of old, but I still recognise the murderous wrinkles on the brow of the old scarlet-robed hag. She may clothe herself in her finest attire, but underneath the gorgeous robes I see the leprous garments of her whoredom.'

The paper's frequent use of sexual imagery reflected a strain familiar in historical puritanism. Nuns, in particular, seem to have inflamed the contributors' imaginations.

Any resident of or visitor to Belfast or Dublin may have noticed of late a rise in the number of nuns parading the streets. Their habit or costume is not the typical nun's garb. These modern nuns are novices, or in lay terms, apprentice nuns. One cannot help but admire their physical beauty, but their furtive smiles and glances show that they are not completely instituted nuns. It would appear that the statement made by some local wit is true:

> 'The older nuns are raving
> While the younger nuns are craving.'

The paper rivalled the secular Sundays in its zeal for rooting out vice. All human life was there. 'Do you know,' asked one news paragraph, 'that the nephew of a

Roman Catholic prelate attending the Second Vatican Council during a visit to Rome, saw his uncle unholily seduced by a most unholy woman in the very heart of that most holy of all cities?' A series of feature articles exposed the infidelities of the priesthood in general and one priest in particular who had 'destroyed or scandalised at least 1,000 married and unmarried females by questioning them on most depraved things for the simple pleasure of gratifying his own corrupted heart'. This evidently boosted circulation, since it was followed by a series on 'The Love Affairs of the Vatican'.

Innocently or otherwise, the paper perpetuated some of the grosser misconceptions about catholicism. One edition published a list of rules purporting to be a valid contemporary summary of Roman Catholic canon law: 'The Pope has the right to give countries and nations which are non-Catholic regents, who can reduce them to slavery . . . He who kills one who is excommunicated is no murderer.' Still more paranoid were its fears of catholic subversion of protestant children.

A Protestant mother recently took her child to be enrolled in the Brownie Pack connected to Fort William Irish Presbyterian Church. The lady in charge of the pack refused to enroll the Protestant child. The mother of the child happened to notice Roman Catholic children going into the Brownie drill room. She queried: 'Are these Roman Catholic girls enrolled?' ' Oh yes,' was the reply, 'and we are very delighted to have them'. So the Protestant girl was refused enrolment by the Fort William Irish Presbyterian Church because that church prefers catering for Roman Catholic children who are engaged in spreading the dogmas of 'Holy Mother Church' in the pack. We believe that these Roman Catholic infiltrators are specially chosen and trained to do this job.

The paper reserved some of its ample stocks of brimstone for targets other than the catholic church, notably the permissive society and the media. The mini-skirt was denounced as 'the cause of the serious population explosion facing Britain'. Mary Whitehouse was extravagantly praised for her crusade against 'crime, illegitimacy, venereal disease, violence, infidelity, promiscuity and drinking'. England was dismissed as a country which 'currently wallows – nay, revels – in filth, sin and evil of the most horrible forms. Abortion and sodomy are by law condoned, even encouraged. Divorce, adultery, fornication, sex perversion, rape, infanticide, murder and illegitimacy flourish'. The BBC was 'that vehicle of corruption', Ulster Television was 'noted for its drunkenness, lewdness, immorality and Popery'. Pressmen were

. . . the whirring multitudes of pestiferous scribbling rodents commonly known as Press reporters, newsmen and journalists. This gangrenous population, to be found in every rat hole in Fleet Street, however, are not as perilous as the typhus carriers, i.e. sub-editors and editors. These creatures are mentally flaccid, physically hairless, repulsive and repellant. They usually sport thick-lensed glasses, wear six pairs of ropey sandals, are homosexuals, kiss holy medals or carry secret membership cards of the Communist Party. Most of them are communistoids without the guts of a red-blooded Communist, or Roman Catholics without the effrontery of a Pope Pius XII. Sometimes these anonymous editorial writers are a mixture of the two. Spineless, brainless mongoloids. But, because of it, as maliciously perilous as vipers.

The puerility and verbal violence of the *Protestant Telegraph* consistently exhibited the silliest and most vicious side of ultra-protestantism. Paisley did not invent the tradition: he took it over when official Unionism abandoned it. Later he was to try to abandon it himself, only to find he had sharpened an appetite which others were always prepared to go on whetting.

But if the political structures of the majority community were under strain, so too were those of the catholic minority. O'Neill's attempt to turn Unionism into English Toryism inevitably drew attention to those areas where the transformation was slow, or incomplete, or never begun: the areas of historic discrimination. As these contrasts and contradictions became more apparent, a growing number in the minority community refused to acquiesce in their second-class citizenship. This revolt was articulated by three distinct social groups: the growing catholic middle class, radicalised by its exclusion from power; the students of one of Belfast's few integrated, non-sectarian institutions, Queen's University; and the working class in the catholic ghettos, who saw Paisley-ism, paradoxically, as both a reassertion of traditional repressive Unionism and, more significantly, an example of self-help and self-assertion worthy of imitation. These three strands, joined by the remnants of an IRA which was all chiefs and no Indians, became the component parts of the Northern Ireland civil rights movement, founded in February 1967.

The slogan 'civil rights' deliberately invited comparison with the black liberation movement in the United States led by Martin Luther King. The analogy was a good one, so far as it went. In both cases a racial and cultural minority, the victims of what Americans call WASP (White Anglo-Saxon Protestant) supremacy, were attempting by non-violent agitation to achieve equality of citizenship and status. But unlike Luther King's movement, the Northern Ireland Civil Rights Association (NICRA) was slow to take to the streets. Its first chairman, Mrs Betty Sinclair, a 'protestant' communist with a long record of work for the trades union movement, understood better than most the danger of a civil rights campaign getting stuck in a sectarian groove. The problem NICRA faced in asserting its non-sectarian character was that civil rights in Northern Ireland were granted or withheld largely on a sectarian basis. To fight discrimination in housing was to demand that catholics be given houses which, under the prevailing system, would go to protestants. To fight discrimination in employment was to demand that catholics move into jobs currently held by protestants. NICRA was later to switch its emphasis to demanding *more* houses and *more* jobs, rightly recognising that discrimination breeds on scarcity. But by that time the protestant working class had come to view the civil rights movement as the old catholic enemy in new clothes: 'CRA=IRA'.

The result was a series of increasingly bloody clashes from August 1968 onwards, clashes in which catholics came to be mobilised under the NICRA banner and protestants under that of the various 'Volunteer' forces.

The battles of Dungannon, Londonderry, Armagh and Burntollet were investigated and described by the Cameron commission. My purpose in the rest of this chapter will be to correct some of the inaccuracies in Lord Cameron's account (and in those that have uncritically followed him), and to expand on what little has so far been revealed about the participation of protestant organisations. For participants who were at first concerned to minimise their part in what was universally condemned as mob barbarism have since been more forthcoming as the passage of time has made it possible to represent their actions as pioneer assaults on an up-and-coming IRA rebellion.

The first civil rights march, from Coalisland to Dungannon on 24 August 1968, attracted some three thousand participants. Bernadette Devlin tells in her autobiography how, despite the non-sectarian protestations of NICRA, many marchers sang Republican songs and catholic hymns. Cameron reported the presence of 'several prominent Republicans', including 'members of the IRA'.

Cameron went on to note 'a move in extreme Unionist circles to oppose the march', and named the local MP, John Taylor (later a junior minister responsible for law and order), as telling the police there would be trouble if the route of the march were not changed. The police complied with this request. If they had not done so, says Cameron, Taylor and local Unionist leaders 'would not have discouraged the organisation of a counter demonstration'. But Cameron does not make it clear that, whether or not encouraged by Taylor and his friends, there *was* a counter demonstration.

A fortnight before the march, officers of four divisions of Ulster Protestant Volunteers had met in a house at Bush, near Dungannon. The meeting was convened by East Tyrone UPV, which invited leaders of the Diamond, Portadown and South Derry divisions to attend. The East Tyrone division consisted largely of B Specials, and its activities were frequently denounced in Stormont by Austin Currie, who claimed that it was linked with the UVF.

It was proposed that the four UPV divisions organise a rally in Dungannon Market Square, timed to start just as the civil rights marchers were due to arrive. This was a traditional manoeuvre, designed to provoke a ban on the original demonstration in the name of public order. But no ban was forthcoming from the Minister of Home Affairs. The UPV divisions therefore met again and 're-luctantly decided to recommend via their MP that the march be diverted from Dungannon'. A deputation conveyed this proposal to John Taylor, who conveyed it to the police. On the night before the march, the police ordered a re-routing through the catholic area of the town away from Market Square and the town centre.

The civil rights marchers consequently arrived at Dungannon to find their route blocked by a police cordon. The organisers had difficulty in restraining marchers from breaking through, but eventually a meeting was started. Betty Sinclair called for the singing of 'We shall overcome' but, in Bernadette Devlin's account, this was drowned out by the Republican hymn 'A nation once again'. There was less confusion on the protestant side of the police cordon, where the Volunteers sang 'God Save the Queen' and exulted in a great victory. As the *Protestant Telegraph* put it:

The attempt . . . to lead a miserable crew of Ulster's

enemies under the guise of so-called civil rights from Coalisland to Dungannon Square on Saturday, 24 August, ended in a fiasco . . . On arrival at the outskirts of Dungannon they were confronted by the RUC and about 1,500 determined loyalists – a big percentage of whom were Ulster Protestant Volunteers . . .

Speaker after speaker poured volumes of abuse on the police who, it is only fair to state, carried out their duty without fear or favour and should have been thanked instead of criticised, for in reality they saved these miscreants from the great crowd of outraged Protestants . . . The credit for the reversal of the fortunes of this mangy crowd was entirely due to the efforts of East Tyrone UPV, ably supported by Diamond, Portadown and South Derry divisions UPV . . .

At the termination of the rebel meeting – it was evident that they would make no further attempt to enter the town – the large crowd of loyalists were addressed by a member of the Executive of the Ulster Constitution Defence Committee, who thanked them for their presence and support. The policy of the UCDC, through the UPV, has been and will continue to be to confront the enemy at every opportunity.

The next opportunity came only a fortnight later when the UCDC and South Derry UPV planned a march through Maghera. To their fury, Home Affairs Minister William Craig stepped in at the last minute and ordered a change of route away from catholic areas. Confrontation was avoided and the *Protestant Telegraph* complained bitterly that Craig 'practised the vilest discrimination against protestants'.

A few days later, a civil rights committee in Londonderry announced a parade for 5 October. It was to be non-sectarian, and consequently claimed the right to march through both catholic and protestant strongholds. Ever since the siege of 1689, the part of the city within Derry's walls has been sacred ground to protestants. Now it seemed the 'Maiden City' was about to be raped by papists. This time the counter demonstration was not left to 'Volunteers' alone. The full weight of the entire apparatus of Unionism, official and unofficial, was thrown against those who dared to challenge its power.

The local Unionist headquarters petitioned Craig to ban the march. The Young Unionists threatened a counter demonstration. The general committee of the Apprentice Boys issued a statement on 30 September denouncing the march as 'a cover for the Republican and Nationalist movements'. Strangely, the statement neglected to mention any plans for an Apprentice Boys' 'annual parade' on the same day, at the same time, on the same route. But notice of such a parade – an 'initiation ceremony' – was suddenly forthcoming next day. Cameron made it clear that he regarded this as 'merely a threat to counter-demonstrate'.

Three days before the march, the RUC told Craig that the civil rights parade was likely to lead to public disorder 'as intense resentment had been engendered amongst the loyalist population'. On 3 October Craig re-established his credit with the extremists and announced his ban. On 4 October the organisers said the ban would be defied. And on 5 October a pitched battle ensued as the march was broken up by two platoons of the Reserve Force (the 'Riot Squad') who, says Cameron, 'broke ranks and used their batons indiscriminately'. Some seventy-seven civilians and eighteen policemen were injured. Television sent pictures of the scene round the world, and the Northern Ireland government was never again able to keep its squalid repression to itself. Craig defended himself against the charge that his ill-considered ban had provoked the situation by counter-charging that NICRA was an IRA front controlled by subversive left-wingers.

The order enforced at baton-point in Londonderry was protestant order. The men of the RUC Riot Squad were the paramilitary arm of protestant supremacy. What need, then, for freelance Volunteer groups when their function was so efficiently carried out by a uniformed militia?

But civil rights demonstrations nevertheless proliferated. One in Belfast on 9 October was blocked by a crowd led by Paisley. Then another was called in Londonderry for 19 October. Since this was billed as a non-violent sit-in, it was harder to ban, and in the absence of government action a counter-demonstration was threatened by a body styling itself the Loyal Citizens of Ulster. The LCU turned out again the following weekend to ambush a small civil rights march from Strabane to Londonderry, attacking it with sticks and stones. And a week later police had to intervene to keep civil rights demonstrations and LCU counter-demonstrations apart in Londonderry.

The self-styled 'commandant' of the Loyal Citizens of Ulster was Ronald Bunting, a mathematics teacher in Belfast College of Technology and a former British army officer who had retired with the honorary rank of major. Bunting was an eccentric. In the early sixties he was known as a radical ratepayers' campaigner against the abuses of Unionist councils, and he supported Gerry Fitt in his Republican Labour campaign for Stormont. Then he was 'saved' at a Paisley meeting. He became a 'loyalist' hero overnight in 1966 when he gate-crashed a 1916 commemoration service in Dublin to lay a wreath in memory of British troops killed in putting the rising down. Later the same year he founded a 'Democratic Party', of which he seems to have been the only member. He has re-founded it several times since, apparently without expanding its membership.

Bunting belonged to the Willowfield division of the Ulster Protestant Volunteers, in East Belfast. His Loyal Citizens of Ulster group seems in practice to have consisted largely of UPV and UVF men. Certainly it had no executive or formal structure of its own, and from October 1968 its name was used by Bunting to lend weight to what were in reality his own unilateral actions. There was inevitable confusion between the UPV and the Loyal Citizens, and Bunting did little to correct the idea (popularised by the Cameron commission and repeated by

71

nearly all subsequent writers) that he was Commandant of the UPV – an office he never held. A man of vivid imagination, he told reporters that his organisation had 300,000 supporters. A more realistic estimate would be that it consisted of up to 300 instant counter-demonstrators, most of whom, like Bunting, belonged to the UPV, and many of whom were B Specials.

On 9 November Paisley and Bunting took several thousand supporters to 'recapture' Londonderry. Their demonstration was organised by the UCDC and UPV divisions and supported by the Loyal Citizens of Ulster, the Orange Voice of Freedom (a newly-established militant ginger-group within the Order), Knights of Freedom (another ephemeral creation of Major Bunting), the Voice of Ulster Christian Ladies (vocally the most formidable group of them all), the Independent Orange Order (founded in 1905 by disssident Orangemen), the Apprentice Boys and the Young Conquerors Flute Band. A wreath of poppies was laid at the city war memorial by Bunting and Paisley told the rally that the events of October were 'but the prelude to an IRA upsurge . . . The day when Ulster protestants will have to face the worst IRA campaign in our history has been brought forward'.

The civil rights movement asked its supporters to stay at home. A few stones were nevertheless thrown at the rally and a stink bomb landed at Major Bunting's feet as he laid his wreath. But Londonderry, boasted Paisley, had been 'recaptured from the papist-inspired, Communist-supported conspiracy'.

Next weekend it was the civil rights movement's turn. They called another rally in the city centre, which was promptly banned by Craig. The scene was set with simultaneous challenge and counter-challenge. John Hume declared that the ban would be breached and the Loyal Citizens of Ulster warned: 'No placard-carrying Fenian will be allowed to pass through Derry's walls.' When the head of the march reached the police cordon, four selected marchers scrambled over the barrier in token breach of the ban and the rest made their way through the gates one by one, meeting up again at the Diamond where they successfully held their rally, 15,000 strong.

By now the street battles every weekend were beginning to have serious political repercussions. On 30 October Jack Lynch flew to London for talks with Harold Wilson. Afterwards he commented that 'the clashes in the streets of Derry are an expression of the evils which partition has brought in its train'. In Belfast, O'Neill angrily condemned this 'quite unwarranted intervention by Mr Lynch into our domestic affairs,' and the *Protestant Telegraph* accused Wilson and Lynch of jointly 'plotting against Ulster,' warning them: 'Our fathers had to arm themselves in defence of (sic) previous traitors in Westminster, and it seems as if history is going to repeat itself. Wilson and Lynch will not be dealing with weaklings like O'Neill when they come to deal with the hard core of Ulster Protestants.'

'Loyalist' fears of a betrayal were heightened when, four days later, O'Neill flew to London with Craig and Faulkner. Wilson pressed for reform of the Derry ward boundaries, one-man one-vote, a reformed system of housing allocations, abolition of the Special Powers Act and the appointment of an ombudsman—very much the programme of the civil rights movement. The following day he told the Commons that if O'Neill was overthrown by 'Unionist thugs', Westminster would have to make a 'very fundamental reappraisal' of its relations with Northern Ireland.

Over the next few days O'Neill's cabinet wrangled over Wilson's reform package. Rumours were rife. Keen Paisleyite noses smelt the whiff of appeasement. A *Protestant Telegraph* editorial gave a graphic, if somewhat romanticised, account of 'loyalist' response.

When this hideous policy of sell-out became known to

certain people, secret meetings were called ' throughout the Province. From these clandestine assemblies the feelings of Ulster loyalists were made known to those who would compromise our Faith and Freedom. Contacts were established and many renewed, with sympathisers in the major cities throughout the British Isles. The future of Ulster was in the balance, like the fateful sword; and friends of Ulster in Britain were kept up to date with the latest news as further information became available. The Minister of Home Affairs, Mr William Craig, was quite fervent in his opposition to the weak and the compromising in the Cabinet and Government. As never before, Ulster's Loyalists should prepare themselves – spiritually and in other ways – for a test of their patriotism and devotion. The threats of Wilson and Lynch may be fulfilled sooner than we think.

The 'other ways' in which loyalists were urged to prepare themselves were not detailed.

On 22 November O'Neill announced his reform programme in which the Derry corporation was abolished and replaced by an appointed commission. The programme also contained four promises: to prevent discrimination in housing by making a points system mandatory on all councils; to appoint an ombudsman to investigate central government grievances; to abolish the company votes and 'give consideration to a review of the franchise'; and to review the Special Powers Act with a view to withdrawing provisions conflicting with Britain's international obligations 'as soon as this can be done without undue hazard'.

The proposals satisfied no-one. To the civil rights movement they were mere promises, not all of them new. But much greater was the disillusionment of the 'loyalist' ultras, outraged at O'Neill's implicit concession of any need at all for 'reforms' of any kind. The UPV issued a statement which came close to being a call to arms: 'In face of these present awful and terrible events, when one by one the lights of freedom are going out, we, the members of the UPV, beseech you, our loyal brethren, for the

74

sake of God, our country and our children, to forget all petty quarrels and jealousies and defend our constitution and liberty . . . He that would be free must strike the first blow.'

That same week, another communiqué was issued in the name of 'Col. William Johnston, Shankill UVF'. Curiously, this too ended with the motto: 'He who would be free must strike the first blow.' But the *Protestant Telegraph's* response was more succinct. In heavy type on its front page it told its readers: 'S.O.S. PROTESTANTS ASSEMBLE ARMAGH NOV. 30th.'

This turned out to be a call to counter-march against a threatened civil rights demonstration in Ireland's ecclesiastical capital. Four men laid the plans for the last-ditch stand against the rebels. One was Douglas Hutchinson, a founder-member of the UCDC who ran Armagh UPV division. Another was Frank Mallon, also on the UCDC 12-man executive. The other two were Ronald Bunting and a fellow-member of Willowfield UPV, a small shop-keeper named John McKeague.

McKeague had only recently made his home in Belfast. He had lost no time in making contact with ultra-'loyalist' groups and becoming active in them. Although always denying his own membership, he has never denied his sympathy with UVF leaders or his admiration for Gusty Spence, described by him in 1972 as 'a man of integrity, the leader of the loyalist cause'.

At a UCDC meeting chaired by Paisley on 18 November, it was arranged that Paisley and his lieutenants would visit Armagh the following day to urge senior police officers to ban the civil rights parade. They would also make it clear that if the police didn't do their duty, Paisley's followers would do it for them. Describing the meeting to the Cameron commission, police called Paisley's attitude 'aggressive and threatening'.

Armagh was the first occasion on which Paisley personally, and the UCDC formally, threw their weight behind a policy of physically countering civil rights demonstrations. Local UPV divisions had led the counter-attack at Dungannon and Major Bunting's irregulars had taken the field at Derry, but now the big guns were out.

Not that Bunting was left in the rear. His Loyal Citizens organised a petition against the march, and hedged their bets by pushing leaflets through Armagh letterboxes: 'Ulster's Defenders – a Friendly Warning: Board up your windows. Remove all women and children from the city on Saturday 30 November.'

Two days before the march the police found some twenty notices fly-posted about the town. They had been put up by Douglas Hutchinson and read: 'For God and Ulster. S.O.S. To all Protestant religions. Don't let the Republicans, IRA and CRA, make Armagh another Londonderry. Assemble in Armagh on Saturday, 30th November. Issued by UCDC.'

That same day Major Bunting announced another attraction on 30 November: a 'trooping of colour and cavalcade' by 'Apprentices and Fellowcraft', 'Tubal Cain Group (Masters and Purplemen)' and 'Knights of Freedom'. The first two were invented by the major for the occasion, and the Knights had first been dreamt up for Paisley's Londonderry demonstration on 9 November. The route and time proposed by Bunting clashed directly with the civil rights march, which was consequently re-routed by the police. Bunting then called his parade off, and Armagh was deprived of what had promised to be one of its more exotic spectacles. But the UCDC's plans for a counter-demonstration went ahead.

On the evening of the 28th, Craig made what was to become a notorious speech in the Ulster Hall. It was by now an open secret that, with Faulkner, he had led the opposition within the cabinet to the Wilson-O'Neill reform package. Craig denounced 'this nonsense centred around civil rights,' and implied that O'Neill was less resolute against it than he should be. He concluded: 'People talk about reform. It is time that we hit this on the head. Change there will be, as change is needed in this rapidly moving world to keep pace with prosperity, but reform in the sense of making right past wrongs is not a problem that we have got to face up to.'

Splashed all over the Northern Ireland papers next day – the eve of the Armagh march – the speech was a timely reminder to 'loyalist' dissidents that they still had friends in high places, who approved their intention of 'hitting reform on the head'.

On the afternoon of the 29th, Paisley had a secret meeting with Craig. He had asked to see O'Neill, who had refused an appointment, but the Minister of Home Affairs agreed to an 'unofficial' meeting. According to Paisley's later account, Craig assured him there would be no ban on his counter-demonstration. But the Armagh police were already formulating a plan to keep Paisleyites out of the city.

The police plan depended on total secrecy. Before dawn, road blocks were to be mounted on all main roads to prevent counter-demonstrators occupying the city centre before the civil rights march arrived. But the plan was leaked. That evening Douglas Hutchinson got to hear of it, presumably from a police source. He put a call through to Paisley in Belfast. They agreed that the only way to be sure of getting into Armagh was to organise their supporters to move immediately, before the police got their road blocks into position at dawn. McKeague and Mallon were given the job of organising all the transport needed to ferry supporters from Belfast and elsewhere, and in the next hour calls were made to all available UPV officers.

Shortly after 1 a.m. Paisley, Bunting and Mallon arrived in Armagh with nearly a hundred supporters in about thirty cars. They parked behind the cathedral and spent the night in their cars. McKeague was less fortunate. The car in which he was travelling broke down on the road to

Armagh and he only just made it before the road blocks went up at 8 a.m.

The police then began searching incoming cars. Through the morning they took possession of two revolvers and 220 other weapons, including bill-hooks, pipes hammered into sharp points and scythes. Paisley's supporters got out of their cars and stood around waiting. They were seen by the police, said Cameron, to be 'carrying weapons such as sticks and large pieces of timber'. Dr Paisley carried a blackthorn stick and Major Bunting a black walking stick. The police inferred from the results at the road blocks that some firearms were being carried among the crowd which had gathered.

Three years later, under cross-examination before the Scarman tribunal, Paisley gave his own version of these events. He insisted: 'I did not see any bill-hooks, I did not see any scythes, nor did I see pikes hammered into sharp points.' Nor did he know whether the cars in which arms were found belonged to UPV members. The sticks carried by those who stood with him in Market Street had been 'picked up or improvised on the spot,' he claimed. 'The people looked around for some sort of weapons to defend themselves . . . There was a disused building that was being pulled down and there were pieces of wood and many people got these pieces of wood.' His blackthorn stick, he explained, 'was presented to me by a man in that district and I thought I should take it seeing that he would be there, and that he would be pleased if I had this stick in my hand'.

Despite the roadblocks some 2,000 Paisley and Bunting supporters filtered into the city centre. The District Inspector told Paisley he was holding an unlawful assembly 'because they were armed and giving reasonable grounds for expecting violence to result'. Paisley continued the meeting and the police withdrew, hoping to get the civil rights marchers through by re-routing them. The Paisleyites got wind of these plans and moved on to the new route. The County Inspector finally decided that the civil rights march would have to be halted and barriers were set up seventy-five yards apart to form a no-man's land between the marchers and their ambushers.

When some 5,000 marchers reached the police barrier and were told they could not proceed because of the Paisleyites, there was an angry reaction. Stewards – many of them IRA men – had a hard time halting the procession, but eventually succeeded in getting a meeting going. Beyond the further barricade, the Paisleyites screamed: 'Let them through!' An Independent Television cameraman, according to Cameron, was 'clubbed with a home-made baton which had been lead-filled and taped' – an unusual implement to be found lying around on a building site. The civil rights meeting ended and the marchers dispersed. Later that evening some of them attacked a group of Paisleyites returning to their coaches and were dispersed by a police baton charge. Paisley left Armagh just after 6 p.m., satisfied that he had averted another Londonderry. 'It was my advocacy of a policy of non-violence,' he concluded with satisfaction, 'that got us out of Armagh without trouble.'

And the street confrontations continued. Only four days after Armagh, on 4 December, a riot broke out in Dungannon when some 300 'loyalists' tried to break up the inaugural meeting of the town's civil rights committee. Police were keeping the two crowds apart when, from the cover of the protestant crowd, a gunman opened fire, narrowly missing a press cameraman. It was the first shot to be fired since the UVF murders of 1966; the first of many in the slow slide towards civil war. The gunman was arrested and charged with a firearms offence, but proceedings were dropped under a general amnesty in May 1969.

In two short months from 5 October, Northern Ireland had seen sectarian violence unparalleled since the 1930s, culminating in the re-introduction of the gun. More marches were threatened for December. Paisley had promised to stop them. O'Neill decided to appeal to the silent majority. 'Ulster stands at the crossroads,' he warned on 9 December. If Northern Ireland continued in riot and disorder the union with Britain was threatened. Wilson had made it clear that if Stormont did not face up to its responsibility by pursuing necessary reforms, Westminster might act over its head. Where would the constitution be then? O'Neill also had words for Craig. In the privacy of the cabinet, the Minister of Home Affairs had already begun to oppose Westminster-inflicted reforms by demanding that Wilson's threat of interference be met with a counter-threat of independence. Now O'Neill hit back:

There are some so-called loyalists who talk of independence from Britain – who seem to want a kind of Protestant Sinn Fein. These people will not listen when they are told that Ulster's income is £200 million a year but that we can spend £300 million only because Britain pays the balance ... They are not loyalists but disloyalists: disloyal to Britain, disloyal to the Constitution, disloyal to the Crown, disloyal – if they are in public life – to the solemn oath they have sworn to Her Majesty the Queen.

Craig picked up the challenge the following day, telling a Unionist meeting prophetically that he 'would resist any effort by any government in Great Britain, whatever its complexion, to use its reserve powers over Stormont'. Next day O'Neill dismissed him, telling him: 'Your idea of an Ulster which could "go it alone" is a delusion and I believe all sensible people will see it to be so.'

But events were now far beyond O'Neill's control. His party's hounds had caught the scent of blood and were not to be denied a kill. When another civil rights march was announced by the new People's Democracy group – a 'long march' from Belfast to Londonderry in the first four days of the new year, it was to lead to what 'loyalist' news-sheets later dubbed 'the Glorious Battle of Burn-tollet'. The story has been told, briefly and with many omissions, by Lord Cameron, and at length by Bowes Egan and Vincent McCormack in *Burntollet*. But what these and other accounts lack is the 'loyalist' partici-pants' own proud account of the affair.

The first day was relatively uneventful, though Bunting and a few supporters put in a brief appearance, waving a monster union jack. Then as the forty or fifty mainly student marchers slept through their first night in the Hibernian Hall, Randalstown, a bomb exploded, demol-ishing a Republican monument in nearby Toome.

The bomb climaxed a day of intensive 'loyalist' prepar-ation to harass and eventually put a stop to the march. That afternoon a secret meeting had been held in Maghera Orange Hall at which it was decided to involve the local MP, Major James Chichester-Clark, in the har-assment planned for the following day. Paisley's Free Presbyterian colleague, the Rev. John Wylie, was chosen to lead a deputation to the then Minister of Agriculture at his ancestral home, Castledawson. As John McKeague's *Loyalist News* recalled three years later: 'The deputation headed for Castledawson and Clark nearly had a fit when he saw 2,000 Loyalists at the front gate of his domain. After a long discussion he was told to be at the barricade in the morning to see that the C.R. march did not go through Maghera. And he was there.'

He was indeed, being instrumental in securing the first of a series of diversions by which the marchers were driven on to minor roads where harassment was easier. Egan and McCormack quote the man who a few weeks later was to be Northern Ireland's prime minister as say-ing helplessly: 'There was nothing else I could do. My constituents demanded that I should join them. So I did.' Bunting's men, meanwhile, were lying in wait for the diverted march. That night, according to the *Loyalist News* account, 'Word reached the ears of the Loyalists that the rebels had formed up at the other end of the town, so in battle formation, headed by the colours, and ten deep across the road, the Loyalists went to meet their opponents.'

Finding the enemy on the wrong side of a police cordon, the mob went on the rampage, smashing shop windows and stoning the local hotel where the press corps were staying. That night Chichester-Clark telephoned Craig's successor as Home Affairs Minister, Captain Long, to urge him to ban the rest of the march. Long replied that he would have a word with Paisley and Bunting next day. What Long later described as a 'courteous and congenial' meeting took place the following afternoon. Afterwards Bunting told bemused reporters: 'I have given a request to the Loyal Citizens of Ulster and thank God they have responded – I thank you very much indeed, God – to hinder and harry the march. And I think they have hindered it, and to a certain extent they have harried it.'

That night Bunting and Paisley were due to address a meeting in the Guildhall, Londonderry, where the People's Democracy march was scheduled to end next day. But first, Bunting called a muster of what several months later he was to describe as 'two divisions of the Loyal Citizens Organisation' at the Orange Hall, Killaloo. Here, elaborate plans were laid for an ambush the following day. White armbands were prepared, weapons improvised and a lorry load of quarry-stones were transported to the high ground above Burntollet Bridge, where they were laid out in neat piles.

In the Guildhall that night, Paisley worked up the familiar theme that the CRA was the IRA in disguise. Wylie urged the people of Londonderry to follow the Apprentice Boys of 1689 and slam the city gates shut against the enemy. Then Bunting urged the men in the audience to assemble the following day on the Claudy road near Burntollet. 'Loyalists who wish to play a manly role,' he said, 'should arm themselves with whatever protective measures they feel to be suitable.'

But violence was closer than Bunting intended. As word of the meeting spread through the Bogside, the Guildhall was surrounded by an angry crowd. They stoned the windows and set fire to Bunting's car. Eamonn McCann, then chairman of the Derry Labour Party, was heard trying to urge the rioters that Paisley's supporters were 'just the kind of people we should warmly welcome into the civil rights movement we must build, a movement of deprived people, catholic, protestant or whatever, campaigning against the system that oppresses them all'. But that night working-class unity wasn't uppermost in the minds of the men of the Bogside.

Eventually the Paisleyites had to fight their way out of the Guildhall. 'It was every man for himself,' Paisley told the Scarman tribunal, 'and the menfolk in that meeting broke the chairs and armed themselves . . . and they charged into the Guildhall Square and cleared away the crowd and let the women and children out.' The first blood was spilt – and the marchers hadn't yet arrived in the city.

Before they set out on the road to Burntollet next morning, Eamonn McCann made another attempt to desectarianise the coming battle. He told the marchers, now grown to three or four hundred:

Remember the nature of those who have hindered us during the last few days. They are not our enemies in any sense. They are not exploiters dressed in thirty-guinea suits. They are the dupes of the system, the victims of landed and industrial Unionists. They are the men in overalls who are on our side, though they do not know it yet. The protestant poor have been bullied and bribed to the stupid belief that they are in some way privileged beyond other people, beyond catholic people.

As they approached Burntollet bridge, a young girl

sprang on to the road ahead screaming 'Paisley! Paisley! Paisley! ' It began to rain huge stones, bottles and bits of iron. According to Egan and McCormack:

Marchers ran frantically in all directions for help and cover . . . Some clambered through the hedges in the hope that they might pass unnoticed among the attackers. They were quickly identified by the fact that they wore no white armbands. In many cases they were batoned by members of the police force who were mingling freely with the attackers in the fields. Others kept moving forward in the hope of leaving the attack behind, but ammunition dumps had been supplied the whole length of the road as far as the bridge, so that the attackers could easily run along above them on the other side of the hedge. A side road, known as Scribtree Lane, provided nominal cover for Bunting and a large contingent of plain clothes B-Specials . . . Once the police protection in front had passed on with uncharacteristic rapidity, the marchers were left completely at the mercy of Bunting's assembly. Clubs were used as well as stones and bottles and women were attacked as viciously as men.

To the left of the road ran the river Faughan and several marchers were chased to its banks. Girls were thrown into the ice-cold water and pelted with stones. A *Sunday News* reporter wrote:

I looked back and saw a young woman (she must have been about twenty) lying face down in the stream. She must have been unconscious and the water covered her mouth and nose. She was drowning. I went back to pull her out, but before I got there some men with clubs started hitting her legs. There were long spikes through the clubs and I could see the blood spurt out of holes in her legs.

Ambulances began to arrive to ferry the injured to hospital. A remnant of marchers, many bleeding and some in tears, struggled on to Derry – where, at the approach to Craigavon Bridge, they were again attacked with stones, bottles and petrol bombs. Among the protes-

84

tant crowd was the Rev. John Brown, a district commandant of the Ulster Special Constabulary, whose part, said
Cameron, was 'the subject of controversy'. [Sir Arthur
Hezlet in his official history *The B Specials* advances the
curious argument that Brown was merely 'watching' the
procession and, as a Special Constable, 'had every right to
observe during a riot'. Almost anywhere else in the world
it would be assumed that the job of the police was to
intervene against the instigators of the riot rather than
merely to 'observe' the attack. Hezlet's innocent comment
emphasises that the Specials were no ordinary police
force.] But the marchers eventually got through to the
Guildhall Square where they held a short meeting.
People's Democracy leader Michael Farrell told them:

While we protest with all the vigour we can summon
against the abuses of the system, we must not lose sight of
our real enemy. Since January 1st we have been attacked
and harassed by groups of people who think they are hostile
to what we represent. But these attackers are not our enemies
in any sense. Largely they are the protestant people who are
impoverished under the same predatory system. Impoverished
they are, and wholly misled.

And the violence was still not over. As the meeting
ended and the crowd returned home to the Bogside, a
new riot began between police and the Bogsiders, ending
with an unprecedented police assault on catholic houses.
'A number of policemen,' Lord Cameron found, 'were
guilty of misconduct which involved assault and battery,
malicious damage to property . . . and the use of provoca-
tive, sectarian and political slogans.' One result of this
police invasion was a tacit agreement between leaders of
the catholic community and the Londonderry Commission that the RUC would stay out of the Bogside till
calmer times. That night, 'Free Derry' was born.

As for the men who planned the Burntollet ambush in
Killaloo Orange Hall, their fame was celebrated in a new

Orange ballad, published in John McKeague's news sheet, the *Loyalist News*:

On the 4th January, in the year '69,
The rebels left St Patrick's hall thinking all was fine.
To get to Londonderry was what they had to do,
They little knew what was in store for them at Killaloo.

At a place that's called Burntollet Major Bunting took his
 stand,
And said 'Men, do your utmost to smash this rebel band.
They're coming down in hundreds and you are 72',
They answered 'No Surrender! We're from Killaloo'.

The true blues they attacked them, it was a glorious sight,
To see the hordes of rebels being put to flight.
They ran and jumped the hedges, pursued by Bunting's
 men,
Down fields and 'cross a river, into woods and glen,
They cried 'Have mercy on us, The Lord protect us too,
And we'll never come again to loyal Killaloo'.
When the fight was over the victorious Bunting's men
Assembled at Burntollet, and not a man was slain.
The Major thanked them one and all, and said 'Long life
 to you'.
God bless you loyal Ulstermen who live round Killaloo.

Who were Bunting's men? In an impressive piece of research, Egan and McCormack named a number of B Specials seen in Bunting's forces: Derek Eakin, Samuel Leslie, Noel Leslie, Sammy Cooke, David Simpson, Willie McGuinness, Ronald McBeth, Kenneth Moore, Davy Cooke, Sgt Geddis Fulton, John McKeegan and Herbert McCrombie. Altogether Egan and McCormack claimed to identify 257 out of a total of more than 300 attackers, and estimated that nearly 100 had records of service with the USC.

The two authors made no secret of their sympathy with the marchers (both were members of People's Democracy). But their claims have never been effectively challenged point by point, either by 'loyalist' spokesmen or in the courts. In several small and some significant details they correct Cameron's brief summary of the ambush, and there is no longer much controversy over their broad conclusion:

> The attack was organised locally by representatives of the Orange Order and the Special Constabulary, in close collaboration with some members, at least, of the RUC. It may be that local branches of the clandestine organisation known as the UVF were involved. But the overlap of personnel between these organisations renders such distinctions of purely academic significance.

Burntollet climaxed the 1968-9 series of set-piece confrontations. The Volunteer movement founded by Paisley, Doherty and Spence in 1966 had discovered, in the emergent civil rights movement, an adversary against which it could unleash its muscle power, vent its frustrations and give physical expression to the inflammatory verbal violence of its leaders. Official Unionism, from the Stormont parliamentary party down to the constituency organisations and their related Orange lodges, continued to resist the patently just and progressive demand for one-man-one-vote and the abolition of institutionalised discrimination. In this last-ditch resistance their fire-power was supplied, now as ever before, by a combination of uniformed guardians of protestant order and civilian Volunteers.

Nearly a year before the British army was sent to restore the peace, most of the strands of the coming civil war were clearly visible. The irresistible force of democracy was battering against the immovable object of 'loyalist' reaction. William Craig was already talking of a possible UDI. O'Neill's 'New Ulster', with all its elaborate window-dressing, was a dead duck.

The refashioning of the province in the image of liberal capitalism had proved beyond the capacities of the

Unionist leadership. A new Ulster required a dismantling of the structures of institutionalised sectarianism. That meant conceding the demands of the civil rights marchers, which in turn meant the systematic destruction of the protestant privilege on which Unionist support was based. O'Neill's response to that dilemma had been to placate the minority (and Westminster) with promises of reform, while reassuring 'loyalists' that the substance of these promises would be withheld. But neither of Ulster's threatened communities, minority or majority, were to be conned that easily. That was the message of Dungannon, Derry, Armagh and Burntollet.

O'Neill seems to have understood that the game was up. On 5 January, in another of those lofty pronouncements which marked the eventide of his patrician premiership, he showed that he knew which side he was on when the chips were down. Northern Ireland, he declared, had 'heard sufficient for now about civil rights' and 'foolhardy and irresponsible' civil rights marchers. The RUC – which, as he spoke, was still running riot in the Bogside – had 'handled this most difficult situation as fairly and firmly as they could'. The government would now consider 'further reinforcement of the regular police by greater use of the Special Constabulary'. Parliamentary protestantism had won a victory – of sorts. And it looked forward to more. 'The Loyalists gave them just what they deserved,' ended the *Loyalist News* account of Burntollet, 'and to all Loyalists at this time we say, "Bide your time, it will happen again unless the government of the day takes its stand." '

7 THE UVF BOMBING CAMPAIGN

Four weeks after Burntollet, O'Neill announced a surprise general election. No one was to know that it would prove the last in the history of the Stormont parliament. Brian Faulkner had resigned from the government on 23 January, followed by two right-wing colleagues. Then thirteen dissident MPs issued a statement calling for a new Unionist government under a new leader. O'Neill chose to fight an election rather than go quietly.

Meanwhile there was light relief in the courtroom at Armagh. A substantial number of counter-demonstrators and civil rights marchers had been charged with various offences arising from the series of demonstrations from 5 October onwards. Among them were Paisley and Bunting, charged with organising an unlawful assembly in Armagh. But as part of a conciliatory initiative launched with O'Neill's 'Ulster at the crossroads' speech, the Attorney-General offered a six-month adjournment of all cases pending. Paisley and Bunting, however, demanded to have their charges heard immediately without any adjournment. The courts obliged and on 27 January they were each convicted and sentenced to three months in jail. The following day, when police called at Beersbridge Road to arrest Paisley and take him to prison, they found him in conference with McKeague and Mallon. There was a scuffle in which a glass door panel was smashed, gashing Paisley's little finger (which he claimed was 'almost severed'). Bunting barricaded himself into his home and the police had to force an entry – an event which transformed the Major's attitude towards the RUC. Both men spent a night in jail before being released on bail. Within a week both had announced their candidature in the coming election.

O'Neill's purpose in bringing forward an election which was not due until the end of 1970 was to assert the dominance of himself and his class within a rebellious Unionist party. The struggle that followed was, for the first time in Northern Ireland's history, not a ritual contest between protestants and catholics but a struggle to the political death between antagonistic classes of protestants.

O'Neill rallied the core of the ascendancy, the still enormously influential local aristocracy and landed gentry, behind the banner of 'official' Unionism. Absentee notables made the unfamiliar journey across the Irish Sea to do their bit. The Duke of Westminster travelled between election meetings with an entourage which would not have disgraced an American presidential contender. 'The Duke's campaign,' commented the *Sunday Telegraph,* 'is only one part of the massive pro-O'Neill operation being mounted rapidly now in Ulster. Money is clearly no object. Aristocratic names are being tossed around freely by the Unionists, including the Duke of Abercorn, the Earl of Erne, to say nothing of lesser peers.' Faulkner, for his part, mobilised the Unionist business class, the ranks of middle capital, in an explicit class assault on 'the landed gentry and big money, imposing their candidates at will'. He also made telling use of his experience as Minister of Commerce to paint a picture of impending industrial calamity if commerce were not saved by a government of businessmen who really understood it.

Both factions fought on the Unionist ticket, which hardly made for clarity. Ten of the thirteen dissidents fought as anti-O'Neill Official Unionist candidates, and were opposed by pro-O'Neill Independent Unionists. In addition, Paisley put up six Protestant Unionist candidates, himself challenging O'Neill in Bannside while Bunting fought pro-O'Neill Roy Bradford in Victoria. Altogether there were

90

sixty-seven Unionists of one variety or another contesting fifty-two seats.

The opposition was equally fragmented. The civil rights movement had made old-style nationalism and republicanism seem irrelevant to many catholic voters, and several of the movement's leaders now plunged into politics. People's Democracy also put up eight candidates, including Bernadette Devlin against Major Chichester-Clarke and Michael Farrell against O'Neill and Paisley. The class war within the protestant community was thus mirrored by an ideological struggle for the allegiance of the catholic voter.

O'Neill's gamble failed. Although by retaining control of the Unionist machine he prevented a substantial sector of the business class from deserting to Faulkner, the crucial objective of establishing a clear dominance within the party was beyond his reach. Of thirty-six official Unionists elected, twelve were intransigently anti-O'Neill and the loyalty of half of the remainder was unreliable. The struggle would clearly continue within a party now divided not only at parliamentary level but also in the constituencies, where anti- and pro-O'Neill machines existed alongside each other in a state of war. Moreover, Paisley had come within an ace of unseating the prime minister in a constituency which had not been contested for a generation. O'Neill survived on a humiliating minority vote, polling 7,745 votes to Paisley's 6,331 and Farrell's 2,310. Four of the other five Protestant Unionists took second place and only Bunting, who was beaten to second place by Labour, failed to poll a spectacular total for the Paisleyites.

On the opposition front, John Hume and Ivan Cooper defeated old-style Nationalists by fighting as civil rights independents. PD came within 220 votes of unseating a Nationalist in South Down and polled substantially elsewhere, confounding those who argued that the conservative catholic working class would never opt for socialism.

91

For the first time in twelve general elections since the founding of the state, class alignments had begun to threaten the sectarian divisions which had so long distorted Northern Ireland's political development.

O'Neill had failed to win, but he had not lost. He was still prime minister. Paisley's supporters found themselves faced with the bitter fact that, after all their campaigning, parading, counter-marching and electioneering, their arch-enemy was still in charge of the province. Their defeat seemed all the more complete when, their parole over, Paisley and Bunting went back to prison and O'Neill confidently assured television interviewers that 'Paisleyism is dead'.

Parades had failed. Politics had failed. In their despair, some 'loyalists' now turned to a more desperate means of ridding Ulster of the one man whose weakness, they believed, threatened their own precarious supremacy. At five minutes to four on the morning of Sunday 30 March, four explosions wrecked the electricity sub-station at Castlereagh in the suburbs of Belfast. Early in the morning on Sunday 20 April, there were two more explosions. At the Silent Valley reservoir in county Down, control valves and supply pipes were damaged, cutting off two-thirds of Belfast's water supply. At Kilmore, county Armagh, an electricity pylon was damaged and a high-tension wire severed. Just after midnight on the night of 23 April an explosion at Templepatrick, county Antrim, fractured a water supply pipe running from Lough Neagh to Belfast. The following night an eighth blast severed a water-pipe at Annalong, near the Silent Valley.

The bombings were widely assumed to be the work of the IRA or other Republican extremists. Certainly this was the *Protestant Telegraph's* assumption. On 5 April, after the Castlereagh explosions, the paper reported:

This is the first act of sabotage perpetrated by the IRA since the murderous campaign of 1956 . . . Suggestions have been made that an IRA splinter-group – Saor Uladh – was

92

responsible for the blast, but the sheer professionalism of the act indicates the work of the well-equipped IRA . . . This latest act of IRA terrorism is an ominous indication of what lies ahead for Ulster. This Province has continuously been subjected to IRA barbarism, especially sabotage and ambush. Loyalists must now appreciate the struggle that lies ahead and the supreme sacrifice that will have to be made in order that Ulster will remain Protestant.

But a month later, after the other blasts, the paper developed the story on a different tack:

A source close to government circles has informed us that the secret dossier on the Castlereagh electricity sub-station explosion contains startling documentation and facts. Original reports suggested that the IRA could have been responsible, but in parliament no such definite statement would be made . . . We are told that the Ministry of Home Affairs is examining reports which implicate the Eire Government in the £2 million act of sabotage . . . By actively precipitating a crisis in Ulster, the Eire Government can make political capital, win or lose. The facts, we hope, will be made public, thereby exposing the chicanery of the Dublin regime.

Special Branch inquiries were indeed beginning to unearth 'startling facts' suggesting the 'active precipitation' of a crisis. But the clues were not in Dublin. Observers had noted that the Castlereagh explosions occurred on the eve of a crucial Unionist Party standing committee meeting convened to discuss the leadership, while the other blasts immediately preceded the parliamentary party's vote on universal franchise. Austin Currie publicly voiced the private suspicions of a growing number when he suggested the blasts were the work of protestant extremists intending to force a crisis which would so undermine confidence in O'Neill's ability to maintain law and order that he would be obliged to resign.

On 28 April, two days after the last explosion, O'Neill did resign. 'Either we live in peace or we have no life

D

93

worth living,' he told the party. A week earlier Major Chichester-Clark had withdrawn his support in protest at the O'Neillites' endorsement, at last, of one-man-one-vote. 'I fear that our supporters will lose all faith in the determination of the present government,' he told O'Neill. That was precisely the message the bombers had sought to convey.

For several months there was no firm indication of who was responsible for the explosions. A UPV booklet repeated the charge that the blasts were 'a skilfully executed plot, undoubtedly the work of the IRA'. Then on 19 October, a severe explosion damaged a sub-station at Ballyshannon, south of the border in county Donegal. A man was severely injured by the blast and died without making a statement. His name was Thomas McDowell and he was a quarry foreman from Kilkeel, county Down, where he lived near the Silent Valley. The circumstances of the explosion and the nature of his injuries pointed to his complicity in the attack on the sub-station. He was a member of Mourne Free Presbyterian Church and of South Down UPV division.

Police inquiries into the death of McDowell led them to a man named Samuel Stevenson of Newtownards, near Belfast. He was a 46-year-old unemployed driver and a former B Special. In the February general election Major Bunting had appointed him manager of his election campaign and for a time he was secretary of Donegal Pass UPV until removed, according to his own account, for failing to attend meetings.

Stevenson made a statement to the police in which he confessed to having been involved in all eight explosions. He also implicated a number of other men, including McDowell. He said:

I first came into contact with the Rev. Paisley by attending his services at the Ulster Hall on Sunday nights about 18 months to two years ago . . . I got a job at the Protestant

94

Unionist headquarters at 25 Shaftesbury Square helping in the election. During this time I met Frank Mallon from Holywood, who I later discovered was the treasurer of the UCDC. For some time there was nothing doing and then Dr Paisley commenced his campaign against O'Neill. As this had not the desired effect I was approached by Frank Mallon who made several suggestions to cause disturbance in the country to have O'Neill overthrown. Among these suggestions was that some installations should be destroyed. He said that this would cause confusion in the country and bring about O'Neill's downfall, which was what Dr Paisley wanted. He said that as the Attorney-General lived at Castlereagh district that would be a good place to hit. He said he would finance the operation and gave me about £30 or £40. He approached me again a few days later to make sure that this job would be done. I think he gave me £25 on this occasion. I then arranged to have the electricity transformer at Castlereagh destroyed . . . The Sunday after the job was done I went to Paisley's meeting at the Ulster Hall. Paisley himself, however, was still in prison on the Sunday after the Castlereagh explosion. When I was in the meeting both Frank Mallon and Hubert Nesbitt of Hampton Park gave me the thumbs up sign. I know that Nesbitt and his wife run a nursing home. A few days later Frank Mallon came to my house and congratulated me on the Castlereagh job. He suggested that if similar jobs here and there were done it would be in the bag. He suggested that I should do something to cause further confusion and mentioned 'We will do something about the water supply'. From then on Mallon was a constant caller at my house. He gave me money on numerous occasions and on other occasions when I was not there he left money in an envelope with my wife. On two or three occasions my wife opened the envelope and counted the money before handing it over to me when I came home. Altogether I got approximately £200 from Mallon. This was payment for Castlereagh, the pylon at Kilmore and the pipeline at Dunadry [Templepatrick]. Frank Mallon saw me after each of these outrages and said 'Good job, good job,' several times.

This and subsequent statements resulted in four

separate trials involving charges against Stevenson himself and the men he named as participating with him in the bombings. Stevenson's version of events was contested in its entirety by the men he implicated, and the prosecutions against all but Stevenson failed. The records of the four trials are nevertheless worth reviewing for the incidental light they throw on UPV and UVF activities.

At first, Stevenson alone went to trial on 5 December 1969 on charges relating to the Castlereagh, Kilmore and Templepatrick explosions. He pleaded guilty and the trial was brief. Mr Robert Babington QC, prosecuting, said it was clear that Stevenson 'was prepared to create disorder with the object of bringing about the release of the Rev. Ian Paisley, who was at that time in prison, and of bringing about the downfall of the then prime minister'. It was also clear that he was 'connected with the Ulster Protestant Volunteers, the Ulster Volunteer Force and the Ulster Constitution Defence Committee'.

For the defence, Mr Turlough O'Donnell QC asked the court to take the view that Stevenson was 'not the man who conceived the idea, nor had he a mind subtle enough to consider the long-term political implications of his conduct. Stevenson was a tool, albeit a willing tool, a catspaw, of those whose minds were much more subtle than his'. After McDowell's death at Ballyshannon he 'realised that unless something was done, there was the possibility, indeed the probability, that not only would some people die but these would include some of his associates'. Hence his willingness, according to the defence, to make a full statement.

Stevenson was found guilty and sentenced to twelve years imprisonment. Mr Justice Lowry, addressing him on sentence, conceded that 'it would look as though you were not the arch-conspirator,' but added: 'Your actions have no redeeming feature such as misguided idealism. . . You were willing for political ends to create the greatest dissension in the community.'

The second trial began on 16 February 1970. Charges of conspiracy with Stevenson and McDowell to cause the Templepatrick explosion were faced by five men: John McKeague, William Owens, Derek Elwood, Trevor Gracey and Frank Mallon. McKeague had been an attender at Martyrs Memorial Free Presbyterian Church and a member of Willowfield UPV until May 1969, a month after the last of the explosions. In February he had fought a local election as a Protestant Unionist. William Owens was an eighteen-year-old employee and close friend of McKeague's who shared his flat in Albertbridge Road: he too was a UPV member. Derek Elwood was a B Special and a UPV member. Trevor Gracey was circulation manager of the *Protestant Telegraph*. Frank Mallon was treasurer of the UCDC; his brother, Hercules, had taken over the secretaryship from Noel Doherty.

Stevenson's story for the prosecution of McKeague and his friends was that 'people in the Shaftesbury Square office were up in arms when Dr Paisley and Major Bunting went to prison. Outside demos were held to try to bring about their release but as these were seemingly not achieving anything the suggestion was made that something more effective would have to be done'. Mallon, he alleged, suggested blowing up the Templepatrick pipeline. Stevenson discussed this with McKeague, who suggested he talk to Gracey and Elwood. 'I made it clear that the work was to be done on behalf of "the big man", as we term Dr Paisley. When they heard that, they were much more enthusiastic about doing the job.'

Four or five planning meetings were held at Stevenson's house and Mallon allegedly provided £30–£40 which Stevenson gave to McDowell for gelignite. McDowell (the man who had died at Ballyshannon) brought the gelignite in his car and it was transferred to Elwood's red mini. Stevenson hired a green mini, paid for by Mallon. On the appointed night, according to Stevenson's story, they met in Tennent Street off Shankill Road and the two minis and Gracey's *Protestant Telegraph* van drove in convoy to Templepatrick. Elwood had brought an unnamed friend, described as 'an ex-serviceman who knew a lot about explosives'. Stevenson claimed he had driven up and down for three quarters of an hour while the others arranged the explosives at the pipe. They then returned to Belfast. At 8.30 next morning Stevenson rang Mallon to say all was OK.

Under cross-examination Stevenson described himself as 'a fanatical supporter of Ian Paisley'. He agreed that two armbands found at his house belonged to him. One carried the letters 'L.O.' which he claimed meant 'law officer' of the UCDC. The other he described as the insignia of the UVF. Stevenson claimed he was 'chief-in-staff' of the UVF. Asked who appointed him, he said he could not reveal that. Later he described himself, almost certainly correctly, as 'self-appointed', saying he made the armband 'just for show' but never wore it. He denied that he was living in 'a world of make-believe', but agreed he was 'chief-in-staff of an army that wasn't there'. Although an ex-B Special, he admitted having previous convictions for larceny, fraud and breaking and entering. His wife gave evidence that the planning meetings described by Stevenson had taken place in their home and that they were UVF meetings. 'I approved of what my husband was doing because at first I believed what Paisley was preaching.'

Another crown witness, Cyril McBride, a member first of Willowfield and then of Donegall Pass UPV, said he was present at Stevenson's house when Mallon called to discuss the Castlereagh explosions and handed over £30 for hiring a car. But McBride's corroboration of Stevenson's story lost some credibility when he admitted convictions for vagrancy, shopbreaking and larceny, loitering with intent, assault, conduct likely to lead to a breach of the peace, assaulting the police and disorderly behaviour. He had also been sentenced to six months' imprisonment the previous June for carrying a loaded gun in a public place.

The police claimed that William Owens had admitted going with Stevenson to Templepatrick. Owens had allegedly told Detective Constable David Armstrong during questioning: 'Yes. I was there, but I only went along for the drive. I didn't do anything at the water line and I have been worrying about it ever since.' Owens was then alleged to have made a statement in which he said that he had gone to Templepatrick but didn't know what was happening until he read about the explosion in the papers. The statement described Stevenson as a frequent visitor to McKeague's home, where he (Stevenson) 'talked about explosions'.

As the prosecution's case drew to a close a massive blast rocked the Crumlin Road courthouse, damaging an interior cell. The jury were warned against drawing any inference.

Stevenson's version of events was challenged by the defence at virtually every substantive point, though it was not denied that he was a UPV member and a paid worker for the UCDC. Mallon, however, denied involvement 'in any shape or form'. He said that a number of frauds and petty thefts had come to light during Stevenson's period of work in the UCDC office. He had challenged Stevenson, who had admitted 'borrowing' money. Mallon had then told him he would be reported to the next UCDC meeting for embezzlement, with a view to being prosecuted. Miss Marlene Johnston, a typist in the UCDC office, gave evidence that, when Mallon had interviewed Stevenson about missing money and told him he would be reported, Stevenson replied: 'Don't you think that I will forget about this. I'll sink you, no matter how I do it.'

Gracey denied being involved in the conspiracy. 'My main object in life,' he said, 'is simply to preach the gospel, which I do around the district.' He thought Stevenson had implicated him because he had been instrumental in having Stevenson removed from the secretary-ship of Donegall Pass UPV.

Owens denied the statements he was alleged to have given the police. They had been made, he said, after he had been kept in custody for four hours without being allowed to consult a solicitor and without benefit of advice. 'This statement which is alleged to come from me is completely untrue. I have never been at Dunadry [Templepatrick] . . . I am not and never have been a member of the UVF . . . I am definitely not guilty of the charge laid against me.'

Elwood said he had never met McDowell, never been involved in any transference of explosives into his car, never attended meetings at Stevenson's house and had never been involved in any discussions on causing explosions. 'As a member of the USC I took an oath to preserve life and property. This oath I have always faithfully fulfilled and I am opposed to violence.'

McKeague made a statement from the dock denying all knowledge of the explosions. 'I never have been at any meetings. I have never been convicted of a crime before these events. I have always been a loyal subject of Her Majesty the Queen and it is against all my principles to commit any of the offences charged against me.'

It was Stevenson's word against that of the others. One jury had already accepted what he said about his own involvement, but that didn't necessarily mean another jury would accept what he said about the involvement of the others. The jury was warned that it was dangerous to convict on the uncorroborated evidence of an accomplice, and McBride's record ensured that his evidence counted for little. All five men were found not guilty, and McKeague was cheered out of court by a welcoming crowd, led by Major Bunting.

At the third trial, which began on 3 March, similar charges were heard against five men in respect of the Kilmore pylon explosion. Mallon was again one of the accused and the others were William Gracey (no relation of the Trevor Gracey involved in the previous case) and three Portadown members of the UPV. John Love (a sergeant in the B Specials), David McNally and Robert Murdoch (another B Special). Murdoch, it will be remembered, had been cleared of an explosives charge in the UVF trials of 1966.

Stevenson was again crown witness and he repeated his charges against Mallon, alleging he had proposed the explosion and provided money for gelignite. He also alleged that Mallon had suggested Murdoch as a suitable assistant, since Kilmore was not far from his home in Portadown. Stevenson said he had contacted Murdoch, who contacted McDowell, and with Love and McNally they together brought a quantity of explosives from McDowell's house to Murdoch's home where it was 'prepared'. McDowell gave them a demonstration of how to fire the gelignite and Stevenson then drove with the five accused to Kilmore, where he and Gracey stayed in the car while Murdoch, Love and McNally allegedly put the gelignite in place and lit the fuse. Mallon was allegedly told the following morning that the job was done and was said to have replied 'Good work, good work.'

Mrs Stevenson again gave evidence in support of her husband and said she had 'warned him time and time again that he was being used by the UCDC and Frank Mallon to do their dirty work'.

Sgt George Jackson, explosives inspector for the Portadown district, gave evidence that, having examined the scene of the explosion on 22 April, he went to a Portadown quarry where he found a car he knew belonged to Mr McDowell, the foreman in charge of drilling and blasting. In the car he found keys which belonged to the quarry magazine. In the magazine he found 313 lbs of gelignite of a type not used in quarry work, plus detonators, connections, fuse wire and ignition cord.

McDowell's access to explosives was understandable.

But the storage in the quarry magazine of non-quarry types of gelignite was never explained. There is evidence that the gelignite was National Coal Board stock which had been smuggled out of Scottish pits by a group of Orange miners, and imported into Northern Ireland on the public ferry. There followed another instance where, as in the previous trial, one of the accused was alleged to have made a statement to the police which was later retracted. Murdoch was said by Sgt James McKinney to have denied all knowledge of the explosion when first questioned about it. But after further questioning, he was alleged by the police to have said: 'Just after Dungiven Orange Hall was burnt in July, Stevenson and McDowell came to my house with about 40 lbs of gelignite. McDowell showed me how to make a bomb and told me to use it to blow up William Street [RC] chapel. After a day or two I wrote to McDowell and told him to come and take the stuff away. He came in his car and took it away.'

Murdoch retracted this in a statement from the dock. He said he first met Stevenson during Bunting's election campaign at UCDC headquarters and discussed with him and others plans for starting an Independent Orange Lodge at Portadown. But they had quarrelled over money for a Lodge banner. Murdoch said he had made the earlier statement because, after eleven hours of police questioning, he was feeling 'tensed up and revengeful towards Stevenson who had made untrue allegations about me. I made up the story about having a few pounds of gelignite at my home.' He concluded: 'I have been a member of the USC for the past twelve years and during the troubled part of last year I was on duty three or four nights each week, mainly guarding installations and the local police station. Since I became a Christian I have been dedicated to the distribution of gospel literature. I am totally innocent of the charge.'

McNally, Love and Gracey made statements from the

dock in which they said they were completely innocent and had never been members of an illegal organisation. Love said he had been a B Special for fifteen years and a sergeant for twelve. Gracey said Stevenson had probably implicated him because he had objected to Stevenson using the name of the UPV to collect money on his own behalf.

Mallon declared that he knew nothing of the Kilmore explosion. The other four defendants were strangers to him and he had never met McDowell. 'I completely deny, as treasurer of the UCDC, the handing over or passing of any money to Mr Stevenson or his wife.' He repeated his accusation that Stevenson had been caught embezzling UCDC funds and the typist, Miss Johnston, repeated her corroboration. She denied prosecuting counsel's suggestion that she would be prepared to tell lies to help Mallon. On 4 March the jury again found all five not guilty.

The last trial, on 6 March, was brief. Mallon and Robert Campbell of Kilkeel were accused of conspiring with Stevenson and McDowell to cause the Castlereagh explosion. Stevenson was the only crown witness and no new evidence of substance was produced. Mallon and Campbell were both acquitted. Stevenson returned to jail to begin his twelve year sentence alone. One of his fellow-conspirators was dead, others (whoever they might be) were evidently still at large. It is fair to say of McDowell, with the Scarman report, that while 'he had the means [access to, and a quarryman's knowledge of, explosives in quarrying], the opportunity and, if Bally-shannon be a guide, the will to commit these offences', nevertheless 'the only direct evidence is the word of Mr Stevenson'. But as will be seen later, Gusty Spence had other views. The blast in the Crumlin courthouse during the second trial had provided a curious punctuation, and an equally curious postscript came on 8 March, two days after the final acquittal, when the home of Austin Currie – the MP who had first suggested the explosions were the work of the UVF – was badly damaged by another bomb.

The last judicial word on the blasts that brought O'Neill's premiership to an end rested with the Scarman tribunal. Scarman received his commission to investigate the explosion in August 1969, before any charges were laid. The four trials and three sets of acquittals effectively prevented the tribunal from pursuing its investigation. It was therefore 'not able to make any findings as to the identity of those who caused these explosions', beyond the evident fact that 'all five explosions were the work of protestant extremists, among whom must be included Mr Stevenson'. Like Doherty before him, Stevenson was an office-bearer in one of Ian Paisley's organisations. Inevitably, the question was asked: how much did Paisley know of what was going on?

Stevenson implicated him directly at several points. In one of his statements to the police he said:

During my meetings with Mallon at my home and in his car outside my home, Mallon was always telling me to be very careful, that nothing must leak out that Dr Paisley had anything to do with any of the explosions or had any previous knowledge of them. I wanted to know if Dr Paisley knew who was doing these jobs and asked Mallon. He said 'Certainly he does. You have to tell him and you haven't. He knows and he doesn't know.'

Again, an incident was alleged in the course of the second trial which, if true, would suggest that Paisley was not ignorant of Stevenson's actions. Mrs Stevenson gave evidence that, after the incriminating UVF armband had been found in the house and Stevenson taken in for questioning, she contacted Mallon who told her he would 'have to get in touch with Ian'. That night she had accompanied Paisley and Mallon to the police station where they complained that Stevenson was being kept too long without food or drink. Stevenson told the court that Mrs Stevenson left and the three of them – Stevenson,

Paisley and Mallon – remained in the room with two police officers. Paisley asked if he had been charged and pressed the police to stop their questioning for the night. The policemen then left the room, followed by Mallon and Paisley. But Paisley then allegedly stepped back and whispered in Stevenson's ear: 'Did you talk?' Questioned about this allegation during the Scarman hearings, Paisley confirmed having visited Stevenson at the police station but vehemently denied putting any such question to him.

Stevenson made a third allegation which never came before any of the four trial hearings. He told the police: 'The night Dr Paisley got out of prison I went to the home of Hubert Nesbitt, Hampton Park. Mrs Nesbitt brought me into the living room where I saw Dr Paisley, Mrs Paisley and Hubert Nesbitt. The Dr came across to me, put his arms around my shoulder and said "You're a boy and a half; well done, but you will have to lie low for a while." '

Again this conversation was denied by Paisley, who told Scarman: 'I remember once when my wife and I were with Mr and Mrs Nesbitt at their home that Stevenson called at their home, but I was not there all the time that he was there. Mrs Nesbitt made him a meal and I talked to him, but it was not along those lines. I talked to him about his wife and about spiritual problems. But I never spoke about that.'

Whatever may be the whole truth, the UCDC and UPV emerge with little credit. Stevenson was a petty criminal, on the fringe of both the religious and the political wings of the movement, who came to be given a certain amount of responsibility as an officer of the UPV and an organiser in Major Bunting's election campaign. 'When the authorities act contrary to the Constitution,' said rule 17 in his UPV rule-book, 'the body will take whatever steps it thinks fit to expose such unconstitutional acts.' Like Doherty before him, Stevenson took what steps he thought fit. And he was caught.

McKeague has consistently claimed since the conspiracy trials that Stevenson was a police spy, if not an *agent provocateur*. Fanciful as it seems, the possibility that some members of the RUC Special Branch used Stevenson in unorthodox ways is not to be wholly dismissed. Certainly the convenient finding of what were claimed to be UCDC and UVF armbands at his home is curious, given the fact that the UCDC does not have 'law officers' with 'L.O.' armbands, nor does the illegal UVF issue its chiefs of staff, or any of its members, with neatly labelled insignia. There are indications that Stevenson may have been a police informer before he became involved with the UCDC, the UPV and the UVF. But it is not yet possible to investigate this matter further. The Scarman tribunal declined to exercise its right to question Stevenson, and the Northern Ireland authorities have since refused to say where he is serving his sentence.

Stevenson does not figure in any canon of 'loyalist' heroes. But curiously, his accomplice, Thomas McDowell, has been accorded the significant honour of an accolade from none other than Gusty Spence. In one of five tape-recordings made by the UVF leader and smuggled out of Crumlin Road jail in 1972, and referred to later in this story, Spence praises the 'hallowed memory of Tommy McDowell, killed in action with the Ulster Volunteer Force'.

Precisely how the bombings were planned and precisely who organised, financed and (with Stevenson and McDowell) executed them remains a matter of speculation. John McKeague has commented that the prosecution made a mess of its case, fitting the wrong names to the wrong explosions at the wrong time, and putting men in the dock for things they didn't do when 'there were plenty of other things they could have gone for'. Whatever doubt remains, the participation of members or supporters of the UCDC, the UPV and the Free Presbyterian Church is effectively proven. A link with the proscribed UVF is quite clear. As Scarman concluded, 'their purpose was to strengthen the campaign to topple the then prime minister, Captain O'Neill, from power and to secure the release from gaol of Dr Paisley and Major Bunting. Their intentions were realised: Captain O'Neill resigned on 28 April and Dr Paisley and Major Bunting were released from gaol on 6 May under the terms of a general amnesty.' In 1966, protestant Volunteers had reintroduced the gun and the bullet to Ulster politics. In 1969, protestant bombers got rid of a prime minister.

8 THE RISE OF JOHN MCKEAGUE

Almost a year separated the UVF bombing campaign from the series of conspiracy trials in which John McKeague was acquitted. That year saw the rise of John McKeague from a small-time associate of Paisley to a 'loyalist' leader in the tradition of his hero, Gusty Spence.

Some time towards the end of 1968, according to UVF members, the small band of Shankill faithfuls who kept Spence's organisation alive made a firm decision to expand its influence by imitating the communist and IRA tactic, as they saw it, of working through a legal front organisation. The obvious candidate for a take-over was the UPV. UVF members therefore decided to join and work through Shankill and Willowfield divisions of Paisley's organisation.

McKeague – who, as emphasised, has consistently denied being a UVF member while nevertheless making no secret of his solidarity with the organisation's aims – became secretary of Willowfield UPV in March 1969, within days of the start of the UVF bombing campaign. Bunting and Stevenson were also Willowfield UPV workers. But McKeague was soon to see an opportunity for building a new organisation of his own. A week or so after O'Neill's resignation and succession by Chicester-Clark at the end of April, a number of Shankill community leaders convened a meeting in Tennent Street Hall to launch a 'community association'. The ostensible reason was the apparently harmless one of resistance to Belfast corporation's slum-clearance and redevelopment plans for the area. But, the Shankill being the Shankill, this otherwise innocent concern had strong sectarian overtones: the objective was the preservation of the protestant purity of the Shankill by an insistence that redevelopment take place within the existing, time-hallowed borders of the 'loyalist' ghetto, and that families displaced be rehoused in the same area. Since, according to an independent survey, 82 per cent of all Shankill residents had relatives in the area and no fewer than 45 per cent of men and 60 per cent of women had lived there all their lives, there were clearly strong communal bonds which now seemed under threat. And inevitably that threat was felt in a vague kind of way to be linked to the broader threat posed by the IRA-CRA conspiracy.

Any movement that promised to embody the spirit of the Shankill might become a potential power-base for ambitious 'loyalist' leaders. From his home across the river in East Belfast, more than a mile from Shankill Road, John McKeague came to hear of the inaugural meeting in Tennent Street Hall. Although he was no Shankill man himself, he had friends among the meeting organisers, one of whom was Mrs Mina Browne of the 1966 Shankill UVF-UPV. So McKeague was invited to the meeting. When it was over, he was chairman of the new Shankill Defence Association. The principal convenor of the meeting, Fred Proctor, who was later to become a Protestant Unionist councillor, accepted office as McKeague's deputy, but a number of organisers played no further part in the SDA, complaining that it had been 'taken over by outsiders who don't even live on the Shankill'.

From the start, the association's 'defence' had little to do with slum clearance. If ever it was the deliberate intention of the SDA leaders to convert the movement into an armed vigilante force, the events of the following weeks played right into their hands. Throughout May there was a series of clashes between police and residents of the catholic Ardoyne, separated from the upper Shankill by Crumlin Road. At the end of the month, a catholic vigilante committee was formed by NICRA to patrol the Ardoyne borders. McKeague immediately organised the SDA into vigilante groups, patrolling the upper Shankill. By the end of June, as recruitment kept pace with mounting tension, the SDA could boast more than a thousand members. Only weeks old, it was suddenly Ulster's largest and most powerful organisation of 'loyalist' militants, drawing on precisely the same constituency that Spence had drawn on in recruiting for the UVF.

There were more violent incidents, culminating in rioting during the 12 July celebrations. McKeague's vigilantes now patrolled openly wearing crash helmets and armbands and carrying cudgels. The police dubbed them 'McNamara's Band'. As McKeague told the Scarman tribunal later: 'We did everything possible to assure the people that if the police failed in their duty we would protect them. I talked to the people in the street. I became known to each and every one of the people of that area. . . I was on the streets every day, every evening.'

As always in times of tension, the few catholic households isolated in protestant territory, and the occasional protestant family on the catholic side of the tracks, came in for a good deal of ugly intimidation. On 14 July a catholic house on the protestant side of Crumlin Road was burnt to the ground 'while 35-40 police stood nearby, unable, they felt, to prevent it', said Scarman. Next day, four catholic families were driven across to the Ardoyne. Two days later, McKeague told a street meeting that 'papishes' in their midst should be given a one-way ticket to the Republic. What others might see as blatant incitement to intimidation, McKeague himself described as follows: 'I expounded to them . . . that people are welcome to live in any part of Northern Ireland, but what I put over to the people was that if they could not live in harmony, and they were not living then in harmony, it would be much better for them to go to one side of the road or the other where they could have their own environment.'

McKeague not only encouraged catholic families to leave protestant streets, he also pressed protestants in catholic streets to move out. He told the Scarman tribunal that he and Major Bunting had visited an elderly protestant lady, Mrs Martin, who lived in catholic Hooker Street:

We went to the house and told her we were there to help her . . . but she wanted to remain where she was. We put it to her we would give her a holiday and she could decide whether she wanted to go back into the area or not. We were about three minutes talking to the old lady or trying to get through to her, when three very important men arrived with a woman and threatened us if we didn't leave the house we would be shot . . . They officially told us that they were members of an illegal force, members of the IRA.

Mrs Martin stayed put. But a few days later, on 26 July, the house of another protestant lady, Mrs Gilmore, was petrol-bombed. It was assumed that this was the work of catholic intimidators but the circumstances of the burning were curious. Mr Vivian Simpson, Labour MP for Oldpark, told the Scarman tribunal that he had met McKeague and some of his SDA friends earlier that day, when McKeague said: 'Can I tell you that Mrs Gilmore's house is going to be burned?' Visiting the gutted house next morning, Mr Simpson found this sequence of events 'perplexing'.

Intimidation intensified over the next week, with McKeague, in his own words, 'organising swaps' – the exchange of catholic and protestant homes. 'The inflammatory leadership of the SDA provided by Mr McKeague,' pronounced the Scarman report, 'must have encouraged the bullying and expulsion of catholics, even though he stoutly denied it'.

What was the RUC's attitude to the SDA during the period? There is no reason to disbelieve McKeague's claim that the two bodies worked closely together. Preoccupied as they were with the traditionally more troublesome Ardoyne, the RUC saw nothing sinister in helmeted, armed vigilantes patrolling 'loyalist' areas. No inquiry was ordered into the SDA leadership's links with other organisations, nor was there any investigation of charges that the SDA was a front for the UVF. On at least one occasion, nearly forty policemen stood by while protestants burned down a catholic house. Four days later the RUC issued a statement that their inquiries revealed 'no evidence of any organised body of men threatening inhabitants in the Crumlin Road area' – a statement described dryly by Scarman as 'an over-optimistic assessment of the situation'.

But on 2 August a new explosion of violence put an abrupt end to the RUC's 'wink and nod' relationship with SDA militants. That day the local Junior Orange Lodge paraded down Shankill Road. Their chosen route took them past Unity Flats, then a mixed but predominantly catholic complex between the Shankill and the city centre. The SDA placed an 'escort' of 300 vigilantes outside the flats, 'so that the young people could pass without interference,' said McKeague. Catholic residents resented cudgel-wielding SDA men on their doorstep and fighting broke out.

When a kind of peace had been restored, McKeague told his followers to return later that afternoon to see the Junior Orangemen safely through on their return journey. By 6 o'clock a crowd several thousand strong had gathered under McKeague's direction. A rumour was circulated that the Junior Orangemen had been attacked that morning and the crowd began throwing stones at the flats. Within minutes every window facing the public road was smashed. More fighting broke out and in an ensuing police charge an elderly resident was so severely batoned that he sustained irreparable brain damage and died a day or two later – the first victim of a mounting war which was to claim ten lives within a fortnight. Police finally cleared

112

a way for the Junior Orangemen and then ordered protestant and catholic crowds to disperse. Most did so, but
about a thousand men in the protestant crowd refused to
move. According to McKeague, it was decided to launch
'a full-scale attack' on the flats. For the hard-pressed
police, this 'loyalist' defiance of their authority was as in-
furiating as it was unexpected. They hesitated for a
moment, then, as McKeague's men started ripping down a
fence round the flats, they raised their batons and charged.
A thousand Shankill 'loyalists' found themselves at the
wrong end of Royal Ulster Constabulary batons, wielded
with a ferocity that had been reserved hitherto for civil
rights marchers and catholic street gangs.

Driven back up the Shankill, the enraged protestants
turned and showered stones on the RUC, only to be driven
further back by another baton charge, and then another.
Fighting continued into the night and shop windows on the
Shankill were smashed and looted. Next morning, police
were attacked by a group of about 400 men armed with
pickshafts and petrol bombs. Barricades were thrown across
the Shankill and when a police armoured car tried to smash
through, it was attacked with a gelignite bomb. Within the
barricades, more shops were looted, cars were set on fire
and a police water-cannon attacked with petrol bombs and
gelignite.

As McKeague described it later,

The police seemed determined that they were going to
take over the Shankill Road. They brought up armoured
cars and proceeded to batter into the barricades that had
been erected. Then when barricades were broken down the
people spread into the side streets and every armoured car
that went up and down that road received a battering, both
from the right and the left of the road. Then the police
seemed to be mounting an ambush in that they were coming
down the top of the road, and immediately people went to
that area to stop this happening . . . Petrol bombs, stones,
everything that could be got was hurled at the police.

113

Four baton charges finally cleared the rioters, and fire-
men spent the early hours of Monday morning dousing a
number of fires. Seventy policemen and about 200 civilians
were treated for injuries. The loyal Shankill was now a
community in rebellion.

The SDA issued a bitter warning that 'never again would
the people of the Shankill have any confidence in the RUC'
– whose proper duty, it seems, was to stand by and watch
the 'loyalists' dismantle Unity Flats brick by papish brick.
Sharply contrasted, however, was a statement from
Paisley's *Protestant Telegraph* which insisted that 'the
Loyalists of Ulster have every confidence in the gallant
men of the RUC . . . The people of Shankill must distinguished the enemy from their RUC friends.'

Why this sudden burst of solidarity with a force which
not long before had been denounced by Paisley as 'O'Neill's
Gestapo'? The truth is that Paisley's apparent change of
heart merely reflected his need to seize on an issue which
could be seen to distinguish the increasingly respectable
UCDC from the SDA. Paisley was becoming uncomfort-
ably aware of the growth of a rival 'loyalist' leadership
on his right flank. The UCDC therefore publicly announced
that 'The UCDC and UPV wish to state that the Shankill
Defence Association is in no way connected with them,
and that Mr John McKeague in no way represents either
the views or the policy of our movement.'

McKeague had in fact already resigned his connection
with Willowfield UPV after Paisley had, as he put it,
'dropped me like a hot cake' when his alleged involvement in the UVF bombings was first reported. Now, to
emphasise the breach, the UPV announced that it was
refusing to recognise his resignation in order that he
might be formally expelled for 'the policies of violence
and the gun' which he was said to advocate.

But Paisley's quarrel was not with the SDA rank-and-
file. At the height of the Shankill riot, he was heading a
deputation urging Home Affairs Minister Robert Porter

114

to call out the local B Specials to restore order. He must have been well aware that, on the Shankill, SDA men and B men often wore the same pair of boots. A month earlier, after province-wide disturbances, Porter had authorised use of the Specials for riot control, but had stipulated that they should not be used in the powder-keg that was then Belfast. After the Shankill riot, however, he bowed to the pressure of Paisley and others and put the B men on the Shankill in place of the RUC. Thus scores of McKeague's men swapped their crash-helmets and armbands for a police uniform, and long before any IRA 'no-go areas', the Shankill became an independent self-policing enclave.

This, then, was the precarious situation in Belfast when all attention was suddenly switched to Londonderry where the Apprentice Boys were due to parade on 12 August.

The events of that and the succeeding seven days are probably the most minutely documented in Anglo-Irish history, ending as they did in the effective take-over of Northern Ireland's internal security by British troops. But there remain gaps in the story, and some of them can be filled with an account of the part played in these events by the SDA, and by those members of the SDA who were also undercover members of the UVF.

John McKeague organised two double-decker buses to take 140 SDA supporters to Londonderry 'to watch the parade and listen to the bands'. McKeague himself took up position at Waterloo Place where the Apprentice Boys' route took them within a stone's throw of the Bogside. He was well placed to see the first exchange of stones and other missiles, but little else. His buses were booked to return to Belfast at 6 p.m. and they left promptly. So the SDA contingent missed the invasion of the Bogside by the Riot Police, the counter-attack which drove them out again, the use later that night of CS gas and the general escalation which turned a riot into an insurrection.

They first saw something of what they were missing when they arrived home and turned on their television sets. McKeague then concluded that 'what had happened in Londonderry could certainly happen in Belfast'. That same night he convened a meeting in the SDA's Wilton Street headquarters at which the first steps were taken to equip SDA vigilantes with firearms. It was decided to compile a register of local people with gun licences, 'and anyone with any legal shotgun was asked to have this available to stop any infiltration into the area'.

NICRA was also holding an emergency meeting that night, organising 'diversions' to draw police away from Londonderry. Violence spread throughout the province next day. That evening the UCDC met and concluded that Ulster was in the middle of an IRA rising. In the early hours of Thursday 14 August, Paisley led a deputation to Chichester-Clark, pressing him to mobilise, arm and unleash the entire force of Special Constabulary.

Nobody seems to have thought it strange that, despite the gravity of the situation, the prime minister was prepared to sit through the small hours in conference on security matters with a clerical oddity who was the self-appointed leader of a private army of Protestant Volunteers. Nor was it so strange in Northern Ireland: Chichester-Clark had had similar sessions a few days earlier, first with Major Bunting and then with McKeague. According to Paisley's own account of his meeting, Chichester-Clark told him that he couldn't use the Specials on full-scale riot duty in Belfast without risking Westminster intervention. Nor could he call on troops stationed in Ulster, since these were under British control and to use them would be to hand Ulster over to Harold Wilson. There was nothing for it but to hope and pray that the RUC could do the job alone.

Paisley then delivered his trump.

We said that there were many thousands of Loyalists throughout Ulster who would be prepared to give their

116

backing to the government, and we suggested that a People's Militia should immediately be formed. He said it might come to that. Then we said that we were prepared to go out and get names of people who were prepared to place themselves at the disposal of the government in this emergency for any work that the government would want them to do.

In the course of the discussion, Paisley refined his proposal. He argued that the government should first call up all available Specials and then resort to a 'People's Militia' if Wilson responded with any kind of move towards direct rule. Whatever the political risks, he argued, the Specials must be utilised and all restrictions on them lifted. And Chichester-Clark understood that if they were not utilised, Paisley would proceed independently to form his militia.

That morning, the B men were on the streets of Londonderry and Belfast, not in their standard roles but fully equipped for riot duty. It was widely assumed, particularly in the catholic community, that this was a direct result of Paisley's threats. If the truth was more complex than that, Paisley's reputation as a tough bargainer was nevertheless enhanced. But Chichester-Clark was right: the full-scale mobilisation of the B men made Westminster's intervention inevitable. By 7.15 that night, troops were replacing the Specials at the Bogside barricades.

But it was still hoped that troops could be kept out of Belfast, so the B men there were deployed cautiously and without firearms. This wasn't good enough for the SDA. A deputation went to Tennent Street police station at the top of the Shankill and told the District Inspector bluntly: 'If youse are not coming yourselves, will youse give us the weapons to defend ourselves?' Getting a discouraging answer, they made their own preparations. McKeague described them to Scarman:

The men who had said they would come with their legal guns were brought into the area, and these were produced and set up at certain points. Sandbags were set up at Disraeli Street about fifty yards on each side down the street. Sandbag emplacements were put up. A mineral lorry was thrown across the road, and crates and things were built up so that they would stop any intrusion into the area . . . There would be roughly, in all, about six shotguns, placed behind these sandbag emplacements with the order to shoot if there was an attack with guns into that street . . . There was a quantity of stones, etc., ready behind these barricades, and also a first-aid post had been set up in a house for any casualties . . . I had already issued the orders that that area would be defended with whatever we had, and if any incursion into that particular area took place, they were to meet it with everything that they had.

No doubt in direct response to all this, the catholic side of Crumlin Road was barricaded by its residents early that evening. Hostile crowds then began to assemble on both sides of the road. A detachment of a dozen Specials was posted to the area, the constables carrying batons but the NCOs .45 revolvers. Many of the two or three hundred in the protestant crowd were seen to be wearing white or red-white-and-blue SDA armbands. At about 10.30 p.m. the two crowds began to exchange petrol bombs. A catholic betting shop and a pub were set alight by protestant bombs. Then the Edenderry Inn was, in McKeague's words, 'deliberately burnt because it was a nest-bed for the IRA'.

The police decided on a baton charge down catholic Hooker Street. Armoured vehicles smashed through the barricades, and two or three incursions were made, each followed by men from the protestant crowd who tossed petrol bombs into the houses on either side. McKeague boasted: 'The protestant people went after them and gave them a lesson which I do not think they will ever forget.' As the riots spread, the police came under fire from a catholic sniper. Fire was returned with revolvers and an unauthorised sub-machine gun, and in separate incidents police fire killed one innocent man in the front room of his home and another bystander in a doorway.

Shortly after the first incursion into Hooker Street, McKeague received a message to come quickly to the lower end of the Shankill where another riot was in progress. Dover Street and Percy Street, two mixed roads linking the Shankill to the Falls, had been invaded by catholic crowds. One had swarmed into the protestant end of Percy Street waving tricolours and singing the 'Soldier's Song' – national anthem of the Irish Republic; the other was advancing up Dover Street behind ingeniously made corrugated iron shields. John McQuade, the hard-line Unionist MP for Woodvale (and a former boxing champion), was marshalling men armed with sticks and hatchets behind the uniformed Specials. McKeague later claimed that he took charge of 'defence' operations on his arrival and organised an ambush of the catholic insurgents, during which their shields were captured. Behind these shields, the protestants then advanced on Divis Street in the lower Falls, where, says McKeague, 'even in the moment of extreme danger, the Union Jack, the flag of our country, was planted in the middle of the road'. As rioting continued, a protestant was shot dead by a catholic sniper and in a brief gun battle three policemen were injured. Catholics were also driven back from Percy Street by shotgun fire from the SDA.

After this exchange, the head constable sent a radio request for Shorland armoured vehicles, mounted with high-velocity Browning machine guns. Since Brownings fired a spray of bullets capable of the highest degree of penetration, these were extraordinary weapons to be made available for urban riot control. In an action which was to receive the stern censure of Scarman, heavy, indiscriminate fire was directed into the catholic flats in Divis Street, killing a nine-year-old boy.

As the night wore on, catholic homes were systematically petrol-bombed. In Conway Street, running south of the notional 'Orange-Green' line between the Falls and the Shankill, sixty houses were burnt to the ground while RUC men, according to Scarman, stood by and took no restraining action. Seventeen houses were burnt out at the Catholic end of Percy Street, thirteen in Divis Street and twenty-three at the catholic end of Dover Street. In the Ardoyne, 113 houses were damaged by fire and seven totally destroyed. Thirty catholic-owned pubs and off-licences scattered across the city were also burnt out and another thirty-six damaged. By the morning, four catholics and one protestant were dead and nearly 400 people injured, more than 100 of them with gunshot wounds. And still it was not over. Next day another catholic and a protestant vigilante were shot dead and thirty more catholic houses were burnt out. Hundreds of families moved out of the Falls and the Shankill as refugees. There were long queues for trains to Dublin and boats to Liverpool.

That morning all available Specials throughout the province were ordered in a broadcast message by Chichester-Clark to report to their nearest police station, this time bringing their firearms. The last inhibition about using them as a fully-armed force had vanished. But by this time, Ian Paisley had activated his plan for a People's Militia. A meeting was convened in his church, attended by about a hundred men, and Paisley distributed copies of a form he had had printed: the applicant was required to state his 'church connection' and 'previous military or police experience, if any'. According to Paisley, some 5,000 forms were completed and returned within the next few days.

But events had already rendered both the proposed militia and the Specials obsolete. The intervention of troops in Belfast was now inevitable. As Paisley's meeting began, the Second Battalion Queen's Regiment arrived to take charge of the city's security and restore peace, as had been done the day before in Londonderry. It was Chichester-Clark's last throw – and as ill-luck would have it, even this went terribly awry.

On his first night in Belfast, the battalion commander mistook the Falls Road for the 'Orange-Green' line. Thinking he was separating catholics from protestants, he deployed his men right down the middle of the catholic ghetto. Not surprisingly, he could make little sense of the pattern of rioting as it continued through the evening. In this confusion, with the police and the Specials withdrawn, protestants attacked the real 'Orange-Green' line and burnt down another seven houses in Beverley Street and forty houses along the entire length of Bombay Street in the Clonard. To the catholics of the Clonard, what happened on the night of 15 August was proof that the British army was as unwilling or unable as the protestant police to protect their homes. Weeks later it was in the Clonard that the emergent Provisional IRA found its first leadership.

By the following morning a second battalion was in the city – and the first had located the true sectarian boundary. The rioting fizzled to a stop and the peace of exhaustion settled on Belfast. Then the myths took root: the protestant myth of an IRA rising masterminded from Dublin and the Vatican; the catholic myth of a co-ordinated UVF pogrom; and the liberal myth, encouraged by Scarman, of a spontaneous combustion for which only history was to blame.

The Scarman tribunal took three days of evidence under cross-examination from McKeague, most of it on the August 1969 riots. Strangely little of his account, as detailed in the three volumes of transcripts, found its way into the tribunal's conclusions. Scarman chose to emphasise the impromptu, arbitrary, unorganised course of the fighting rather than unravel the actions and plans of specific organisations. But the SDA made no secret of the leadership, organisation and fire-power it provided on the protestant side. There is no reason to suppose that McKeague exaggerated his personal role or that of his organisation. And for months afterwards the private joke in the SDA was a cryptic 'twenty-four hours!', meaning that if the British army had only delayed their arrival that long, the catholic ghettos would have been wiped out.

While they were not in the least inclined to minimise the part they had played in giving the 'Taigs' a bloody nose, the 'loyalists' nevertheless saw the August riots as the outcome of a bloody IRA subversion plot. They expected the newly-arrived troops to restore protestant law and order, by which they meant putting down the catholic rising. Instead, the army was deployed to defend those areas which had clearly been under attack, and could point to scores of burnt-out houses to prove it. Thus the soldiers stood with their backs to the 'rebel' ghettos and their bayonets towards the 'loyalists'.

Over the next three months, a seemingly remorseless series of events strengthened the paradox by which 'loyalists' prepared to fight the Queen's uniform while catholics plied their traditional enemies with cups of tea.

First, the protestant community was angered when, instead of invading the barricaded areas of 'Free Derry' and 'Free Belfast' (the Falls), the Army GOC, General Freeland, chose to 'talk the barricades down' by negotiation. McKeague and his men saw this at best as a proof that the English didn't understand the peculiar dynamics of Ulster and at worst an act of abject appeasement.

Then on 19 August Chichester-Clark, Faulkner and Porter flew to London for talks with Wilson and were forced to face the fact that, with British troops doing the job that Ulster police and Specials had failed to do, Westminster now had the whip hand. There followed the 'Downing Street Declaration' which not only backed the civil rights programme of those whom the 'loyalists' continued to see as insurrectionists, but took the first significant step towards robbing the protestants of their private army. The Specials were to be placed under the command of the GOC and, in Wilson's words, 'phased away from the riot areas'. 'Mr Wilson,' thundered Paisley, 'has capitulated to the hierarchy of the Roman Catholic Church by destroying at a stroke of the pen the Special Constabulary – Ulster Loyalists' last line of defence.'

Freeland immediately announced his intention of taking into army custody the arms of Belfast and Londonderry Specials, leaving only the rural platoons in control of their own armouries. He diplomatically denied that this constituted 'disarming' the Specials. Whitehall called it 'defanging'. Paisley's message became more strident: 'I say to all Specials: "Don't let anyone disarm you." We will take whatever action we think fit to stop the Specials being disarmed.' But the action he saw fit to take turned out to be nothing more muscular than a petition. The disarmament of the Specials proceeded.

More explicit threats were made on the Shankill Road. John McKeague called a press conference and boasted that the SDA had 'hundreds of guns' and rich friends if they needed more. The Association, he said, could put 'a couple of guns and a tank' in every house on the Shankill. 'We take up this battle that has now been placed upon us, and we will see the battle through to the end. What they started we, the protestants, will finish. We are now going to take the initiative.' Major Bunting, who had broken with Paisley and was jointly sponsoring the press conference, added: 'The protestant dog can bark, the protestant dog has teeth and the protestant dog will bite if need be.'

Some of the bark and bite was again supplied by the UVF. By mid-August, at least a score of SDA members were also acting clandestinely in the name of the proscribed organisation. A group of them took a British television crew into the hills above Belfast and, in the anoraks and black hoods which were to become the uniform of thousands three years later, they drilled and carried out firing practice until an approaching RUC patrol was spotted two or three hundred yards away. The public relations aspect of the operation was obvious: the militants wanted both of their enemies, the British army and what was conceived to be the IRA, to see that the UVF was no myth. But while the drilling and the mocked-up training sessions had an air of the Gang Show about them, the firearms were real enough, and so was the deadly serious-ness of those who took part and insisted on a promise of anonymity.

Protestant insecurity, bewilderment and sense of be-trayal deepened. On the day Freeland began his 'defang-ing' operation, the Westminster government announced the appointment of an advisory committee on reorganisa-tion of the Northern Ireland police, under Lord Hunt. A week later came the announcement of a judicial inquiry into the riots, to be chaired by Mr Justice Scarman. And Cameron, whose commission on the earlier riots had been boycotted by Craig, Paisley and Bunting, had still to report.

Meanwhile the catholic ghettos remained barricaded, negotiations between the army and vigilante leaders having stuck on the vigilantes' insistence that no RUC men would ever again be allowed into the Falls. On 3 September, John McKeague showed what he meant by a protestant initiative. That night barricades were erected all along the Shankill in an operation which was to be dramatically copied by the UDA three years later. They were 'token barricades', said McKeague, and they would come down when the army put an end to the catholic no-go areas. Till then the Shankill too would be no-go to the army. In the back room of a tiny terraced house belonging to a member of the Spence family, 'Radio Free Shankill' began broadcasting a non-stop programme of Orange songs and vigilantes' requests, using a transmitter built from components 'borrowed' from the BBC.

Freeland now felt obliged to move against the catholic

124

barricades, and army bulldozers began tearing at the burnt-out buses and piles of paving stones. At first they met little opposition, but on 7 September, a Sunday, it was reported that a catholic house in Beverley Street had come under attack by protestants within hours of the local barricades being torn down. A crowd gathered from the Falls, whereupon McKeague made a dramatic broadcast on Shankill radio, urging his people to take to the streets to repel a 'rebel and Republican invasion'.

Within minutes two thousand men were converging on Beverley Street, many of them armed. But the army, which had monitored McKeague's broadcast, was there before them. Refusing orders to disperse, the protestants began stoning the troops and were treated to a barrage of what they themselves had derisively called 'Londonderry Air' or 'Bogsiders' Delight': CS gas. As news that the army and the Shankill were fighting it out spread through Belfast, a crowd from 'loyalist' Sandy Row formed up and rushed army positions, dragging away barbed-wire road-blocks to barricade their own streets.

It was the first pitched battle since the army's arrival in the province. And it was the 'loyalists', not the 'rebels', who were the army's attackers.

Next day an SDA vigilante was shot dead, almost certainly by a catholic sniper. The barricades on both sides were strengthened again, and the price the army had to pay for talking them down was the construction of the so-called 'Berlin Wall' along the Falls-Shankill Orange-Green line, and a guarantee that troops would stand guard against further protestant incursions.

With protestant morale still dangerously low, publication of the Cameron report depressed it further. The commission upheld civil rights charges of Unionist gerrymandering and discrimination, and documented them more authoritatively than NICRA could ever do. While it deplored the influence of 'subversive left-wing and revolutionary elements' in the civil rights movement, its most scathing criticisms were reserved for Paisley, Bunting and the UPV divisions for 'inflaming passions and engineering opposition to lawful, and what would in all probability otherwise have been peaceful, demonstrations'. Craig's assessment of the civil rights movement as a Republican front – the cornerstone of the protestant case – was dismissed as 'dangerously superficial and erroneous'; and, most important, the commission roundly declared that implementation of the reform programme was essential to the peace of the province. To the 'loyalists', it was clear that the rebels were winning the propaganda battle hands down.

Paisley was far from silent all this time. In September he prepared a 20-point memo to Callaghan, advising him among other things that 'the high incidence of unemployment in the North, and the shortage of houses, can be attributed exclusively to the Papist population. These people breed like rabbits and multiply like vermin.' Later in the month he did a quick tour of the southern bible-belt states of the USA where, feeding the prejudices of his hosts, the Bob Jones University, he neatly switched the emphasis of his attack from Romanism to communism. 'May God open our eyes,' he told his receptive audiences of George Wallaceites, 'to see the conspiracy, the international conspiracy that is amongst us! May he help us to see that there is a deliberate association of attacks against law and order and for revolution and anarchy and Marxism in the land.'

Paisley brought Dr Bob Jones Jun. back to Belfast to officiate at the opening of his vast new Martyrs Memorial Church, built at a cost of £200,000. A mile from the crumbling, slum-surrounded mission at Albertbridge, it occupied a site in respectable, semi-detached, lace-curtain territory, catering for a petty bourgeoisie which looked to religion for the security which the working class found in the solidarity of their ghettos. Political Paisleyism was proletarian, but religious Paisleyism attracted lower middle class congregations which crammed the ample car park with their Cortinas. 'Do film the cars driving in,' a television crew was told by Mr Gunning, the church secretary. 'It will show that we're getting a better class of person.'

The first Sunday services in the new church were scheduled for 5 October. An inaugural service for Orangemen was arranged for the afternoon (although Paisley himself had left the Order in protest at its apostasy). A number of Orangemen let it be known that they intended to parade to the church in defiance of a government ban on parades. One of the organisers of the procession was John McKeague.

The planned route took the parade through a sensitive area of East Belfast which had so far been uncharacteristically trouble-free. The army cordoned off the road, and when some of the Orangemen tried to break through they were dispersed with CS gas. Rioting spread across East Belfast and when darkness fell troops came under fire from protestant snipers. It was the second violent confrontation between the army and 'loyalists'.

The third and bloodiest was the following weekend. On Friday 10 October the government published the Hunt report, recommending that the B Specials be replaced by a non-sectarian Ulster Defence Regiment, the RUC disarmed and the police authority revamped to give proportional representation to catholics. 'The Specials are not being disbanded,' an ashen-faced Chichester-Clark told the press, 'only their name and organisation will change.'

That night the SDA met and drafted a statement which ended: 'A day is fast approaching when responsible leaders and associations like ourselves will no longer be able to restrain the backlash of outraged Loyalist opinion.' That backlash was to break the following day. Saturday night is drinking night on the Shankill. As the bars closed, angry crowds began to gather at Unity Flats. Sir Arthur Young, who had just spent his first day in Belfast as the new police chief, later described what he saw that night: 'They rose in their wrath to demonstrate against the vile things Hunt had said about their wonderful police. They came in their thousands down the Shankill, appearing like animals, as if by magic. Then they marched to burn the catholics out of the nearby flats.'

Just after midnight, new barricades were built across Shankill Road and on Conway Street, North Howard Street and Malvern Street, sealing off the entire area. Police and B Specials were called up to push the crowd back, and when they proved unsuccessful, a platoon of soldiers moved in and fired CS gas. A detachment of RUC men moved in line down Townsend Street and from the protestant crowd a sniper opened fire. Constable Victor Arbuckle fell dead and two other policemen were injured. Arbuckle was the first RUC man to die in the riots – killed by 'loyalists' demonstrating against his disarmament.

More troops moved in and the sniping intensified. The army claimed that over a thousand rounds were fired at them, including bursts from at least one machine-gun and several sub-machine guns. Fire was returned and two civilians were shot dead. There is evidence that an IRA contingent from the Ardoyne joined in the shooting, fighting for a time alongside the SDA snipers. Other protestant ghettos in the city began rioting in sympathy with the Shankill. In North Belfast, troops drove back a mob intent on burning a catholic church. Across the river in East Belfast, police were stoned and fired on by more snipers. By dawn on Sunday, casualty figures totalled three dead and sixty-six injured. Army snatch squads made sixty-nine arrests, many of them with extraordinary violence. Houses were smashed into by troops and their occupants beaten up. One man arrested had both arms broken, another a fractured skull. Several were released by the courts when they successfully complained of army brutality or exposed gaping inconsistencies in the army's evidence.

On Sunday the army mounted a massive arms search

throughout the Shankill. The results highlighted a sinister anomaly: arms there were in plenty but nearly all were held legally under licence. Records were closely guarded by the RUC but it was estimated that there were 102,000 licensed guns in Ulster, almost all in protestant hands.

But the guerilla anti-search techniques that were later to be associated with the Falls and Ballymurphy were pioneered that weekend on the Shankill: the banging of bin lids to give warning of a squad's approach, the deployment of densely packed crowds of women and children to harass and slow the army's advance from house to house. The SDA even organised the digging of an anti-tank pit and filled it with petrol, ready to be fired if armoured cars attempted to pass.

The bloody weekend of 11-12 October put the seal of a bitter enmity on relations between the British army and 'loyalists'. It was the third major clash between them since the troops had arrived: no such confrontation had yet taken place with the catholics. The army's rugged methods of riot control and arrest had been demonstrated – on protestants. The army's first house-to-house search had been carried out – in protestant homes. It was the 'loyalist' population, loyal to the British connection, which now denounced British troops as a foreign army of occupation. And, not for the last time, it was William Craig who faced up to the UDI implications of such an attitude. If necessary, he told a Young Unionist meeting on 21 October, Ulster would have to go it alone – 'and I would not rule out the use of arms'.

On the Sunday night after Arbuckle was killed, John McKeague attended Paisley's church for a special UPV service. Paisley asked him to leave, and the breach between them was complete. Three days later McKeague joined Gusty Spence in Crumlin Road jail, sentenced to three months for his part in organising the illegal parade to Paisley's inaugural service.

In Shankill Road and East Belfast, there was no shortage of Volunteers to take his place and continue his work.

9 ENTER THE UDA

It was a topsy-turvy world in which the British army
fraternised with republicans and fought 'loyalists'. There
could be no permanence to such a situation. The army's
role was, first, the protection of catholic ghettos, and
second, the restoration of law and order. And therein lay
an irreconcilable contradiction. For in Ulster, law was
protestant law and order protestant order.

Six months after the army's arrival, the reform package was still nothing more than a parcel of promises. The
anger and frustration which had fired the civil rights
movement began to be re-kindled in the catholic community. In March 1970 there were a series of skirmishes
between catholic crowds and troops, culminating in a full-
scale riot in Ballymurphy on 2 April. Freeland announced
that there were circumstances in which he would authorise troops to 'shoot to kill', and veteran Nationalist Party
leader Eddie McAteer declared that British soldiers would
no longer be welcome in catholic homes. Paisley's *Protestant Telegraph* noted this return to familiar normality:
'While Protestants suffered harshly and unduly from the
military, it is obvious that the security forces must be
maintained to defend unequivocally the State and the
loyal Protestant majority against a rebel minority.'

Paisley claimed that the Ballymurphy riots were 'inspired by the Provisionalists', and he may well have been
right in substance if not in name. Derided in the ghettos
for their inability to defend the catholic areas in August
1969, the IRA had regrouped, recriminated and split.
Financed, as it transpired, by sympathisers in high places
in Dublin, the Provisional wing was recruiting and re-

arming in the no-go areas British troops were protecting. Why should the 'loyalists' be allowed to steal their rebel traditions?

The inevitable re-emergence of traditional alignments was hastened by the Conservative victory in the Westminster general election in June. Both parliaments having jurisdiction over Northern Ireland were now controlled by the one Conservative and Unionist Party. Paisley, too, had won a Westminster seat barely two months after capturing O'Neill's old Stormont seat.

Heath and Home Secretary Maudling were content to leave the running of Ulster's affairs, including security, to their political kith and kin in Belfast. Their first action on taking office was to turn down an appeal by Freeland, who wanted them to overrule a decision by Chichester-Clark's Joint Security Committee to allow the July Orange parades to go ahead. In riots the following weekend, more died in Belfast than had died in August 1969.

First, two protestants were killed in a sectarian exchange of gunfire in West Belfast. As riots spread through the city, an East Belfast UVF unit attacked a catholic church in Newtownards Road with petrol bombs, burning down the adjoining sexton's. house. The Provisional IRA rallied to the defence of the church and the protestants returned with guns. There followed the first recorded gun battle between the IRA and the UVF. It lasted six hours through the night, and by dawn two protestants had been shot dead and another two, possibly by-standers, fatally wounded.

Frantic attempts were made by Republican Labour MP Paddy Kennedy to persuade the army to intervene, but all available troops were said to be engaged in riot control elsewhere. Their failure to put in an appearance when told of the initial petrol bomb attack on the church convinced catholics that their former protectors were now under new political management and that henceforth they must look to themselves alone for protection.

The protestants, on the other hand, interpreted the weekend's riots as a sign that the army was either unable or unwilling to create conditions in which they could peacefully enjoy their traditional demonstrations of ascendancy. In particular, they resented the impartiality with which the army's snatch squads made their often brutal arrests. A protestant sentenced to five years imprisonment for 'possessing a petrol bomb with intent to endanger life' wrote in jail an account of his arrest which pre-dated by more than a year almost identical brutality stories from catholic internees.

Captured by the British army, arms and legs held by six soldiers, another two placed in front of me, the other behind. The first blow with the baton delivered with full force strikes me across the top of my eye, blinding me. Almost at the same time a similar blow to the back of my head opens it up like a crushed egg. I can feel the blood thick, hot and sticky cascading down my neck and back. They keep it up, blow after blow delivered with full force . . . I had a huge swelling of the forehead and above both eyes, both eyes blackened, both lips split, two teeth knocked out and skin completely torn off my back from neck to waist.

One result of this tripartite violence was a renewed call from Paisley and his Stormont side-kick, Rev. William Beattie, for a People's Militia. At a private meeting in the prime minister's rooms on 28 June, Chichester-Clark told them he was sympathetic: in the new political climate, it might be possible to mobilise such a force. Beattie, unable to contain himself, gleefully told supporters that the government had been forced to bring back the B Specials, and an unhappy Chichester-Clark found himself trying simultaneously to confirm the story for his hard-line supporters and deny it for the opposition. 'I am not envisaging some sort of armed force or anything of the kind that is going to take drastic action,' he told Stormont. 'I am envisaging some type of organisation which is going to have some authority behind it and which can perform a useful role in the task of helping to keep the peace . . . This is still something that is very much in embryo form.' But at the next Joint Security Committee meeting Freeland saw to it that the embryo was promptly aborted, and this time Westminster backed his judgment.

In compensation for this exercise of his veto in security matters, Freeland agreed at the same meeting to Chichester-Clark's demands for a new 'get tough' policy by the army. 'Exemplary force' was to be used against future rioters, and arms searches were to be carried out in the catholic no-go areas. Two days later, on 3 July, troops cordoned off Balkan Street in the Lower Falls and searched every house. The Falls erupted and was soon smothered in CS gas. Nail bombs and petrol bombs were hurled at the troops, five of whom were injured by home-made grenades. Then the army was fired on – and re-turned a massive 1,500 rounds. Three civilians were shot dead and thirty wounded. A fourth civilian was run down and killed by an armoured car. The catholic Central Citizens Defence Committee alleged 277 separate cases of army 'damage, theft, misconduct and brutality' (and the army admitted to ripping up floor boards and other dam-age in some sixty cases). A curfew was put on the area (illegally, as it transpired) and all movement in and out was restricted for three days. The army picked up twenty-eight rifles, fifty-two pistols, twenty-four shot-guns, two carbines and 20,000 rounds of ammunition – a small haul by later standards. But they severed what remained of their friendly relationship with the catholic community. A month later a twenty-one-year-old docker was jailed for six months for painting 'No Tea Here' on the wall of his house.

The Orange parades on 12 July went ahead behind the heaviest escort in their history, with the army committed to the biggest combined operation on British territory since the second world war. Then Chichester-Clark banned all further parades for six months, only to see the ban defied by protestant militants. Ten men, including John McQuade MP and the Rev. William McCrea, a Free Presbyterian minister, were fined £20 each for marching illegally to a Paisley service on 1 August. McQuade was one of eight men fined between £10 and £15 for illegal assembly on the Shankill on 12 August. Another ten were fined between £10 and £25 for an illegal parade at Bangor, and six members of the Royal Black Preceptory – the cream of Orangemen – were given six month jail sentences for organising a Black march in Lurgan. By the end of the summer, protestant anger and frustration remained as intractable as catholic revolt.

Both sides were busily stockpiling hardware. IRA guns were being brought across the border, UVF guns from Scotland. Some of the protestant guns came in small consignments smuggled in by the militant 'loyalists' who dominate the fishing fleet based at Kilkeel. When a Royal Navy patrol boat intercepted and searched several boats in the fleet, Paisley made a public protest. But protestant gun-running was as yet on a modest scale. There was no lack of licensed guns on the Shankill, and many of the weapons formerly in the hands of the B Specials were now with the SDA.

There was also gelignite smuggling that summer. Some of it, according to one UVF source, came from Scottish Orangemen working in coal mines near Edinburgh. A stick or two could be saved at each shot-firing and brought to the surface in a lunch-bag. When enough had been collected to fill a suitcase, it was carried into Ulster on the Stranraer-Larne ferry. A year later the IRA was using the same route, working with catholic sympathisers in the same group of mines. When it was clear that there was an appreciable wastage of gelignite, the NCB imposed a more rigorous checking system – by which time the IRA, at least, was tapping a more abundant source in quarries south of the border. By the end of 1970 there had been a number of isolated explosions in Belfast, most of them the work of the IRA, but at least two – the courthouse blast during McKeague's trial and the blowing up of 'Roaring Hanna's' statue, hopefully to spark off a backlash – the responsibility of 'loyalist' extremists.

The single factor which more than any other inflamed 'loyalist' opinion was the continuing, open existence of catholic no-go areas, enclaves where the Queen's writ was not allowed to run. To the protestant mind, these were islands of subversion which they would have destroyed for all time had not the British army misguidedly intervened in August 1969. For well over a year, in their view, the army had pussy-footed about, now playing tough with an arms search, now openly negotiating with known IRA leaders, and all the time refusing protestant demands for a full-scale, bloody invasion.

By the start of 1971 it was clear to Chichester-Clark that he would be submerged by the fury of his own supporters unless he found a quick solution to the no-go problem. Rank-and-file Unionists had to be reassured that things were not as bad as they seemed. Chichester-Clark accordingly told them that what the IRA claimed as no-go areas were simply small groups of streets where police access was subject to 'temporary restriction', self-imposed by the RUC, not enforced by the IRA.

Unfortunately for the prime minister, renewed rioting in Ballymurphy ended in the establishment of a new no-go area in Belfast's biggest housing estate. When Chichester-Clark again denied that there was any part of the city which the RUC could not visit if they so wished, preparations were put in hand to expose the frailty of his claim. On the night of 14 January two RUC men patrolling the borders of the Provisional stronghold of the Clonard walked into the no-go area on hearing what they described as a suspicious noise in Kashmir Road. A group of vigilantes soon put them out. They waved down an army patrol, told them what had happened and asked for assistance. But according to the two policemen, the sergeant in charge of the army patrol told them he had orders that no police were to be allowed into the area. More explosively, he added that there was an agreement between the army and local IRA leaders to that effect.

The two policemen made their reports next morning. Mysteriously, copies found their way to Craig and Paisley. That same day Paisley also came into possession of a secret RUC Special Branch briefing which, despite what the prime minister was saying, clearly acknowledged the existence of no-go 'safe areas' for the IRA. Paisley took both documents to Chichester-Clark's private secretary, Brian Cummings, who warned him that the Special Branch report was classified. Paisley replied that he nevertheless proposed to read it into the record of a forthcoming law and order debate in Stormont, under the protection of parliamentary immunity. He did so on 27 January, and Chichester-Clark's pretence that there were no no-go areas was finally shattered.

Forced to reassert its authority, and to be seen to be doing so, the British army began house-to-house searches in the Clonard on 3 February. Fighting broke out as the troops met resistance. At lunch time, several hundred protestant workers from the nearby Mackie's foundry joined the troops and pelted catholics with 'Belfast confetti' – nuts, bolts, ball-bearings and general machine-shop waste. Full-scale rioting spread to the Falls, the Ardoyne and New Lodge, where an army jeep knocked down and killed a three-year-old girl. After three nights of continuous rioting and gun battles, Gunner Robert Curtis was shot dead, the first British soldier to be killed in battle in Northern Ireland since the 1920s. That same night a nineteen-year-old Provisional IRA officer and an IRA volunteer died. Next day Chichester-Clark went on tele-

136

vision to declare: 'Northern Ireland is at war with the Irish Republican Army Provisionals.'

John McKeague's Shankill Defence Association proceeded to carve out for itself a role in the war. In the next three weeks gun clubs were formed under SDA auspices in the Shankill, Oldpark, Crumlin and Glencairn areas. McKeague's *Loyalist News* urged readers to prepare for 'a holocaust which will make August '69 look like a Sunday picnic'. A protestant arms dealer and ex-B Special, Robert Kane, was charged with unlawfully supplying 'loyalist' groups, and on 19 April was given a 12-month suspended jail sentence. Most of the weapons he supplied were never traced.

But it was the Provisionals who now took the offensive and thereby changed the whole character of the Northern Ireland 'problem'. On 26 February an RUC Special Branch inspector and a constable were shot dead in a Belfast street. Two days later an army lance-corporal died when a patrol was ambushed and petrol-bombed in the Bogside. Then on 10 March, three off-duty Scottish soldiers were found murdered in a country lane west of Belfast. That weekend 8,000 protestant workers took to the streets to demand either internment of IRA members or the resignation of Chichester-Clark.

The marchers were led by a sixty-year-old Shankill militant who was to play an increasingly prominent part in 'loyalist' affairs. 'King' Billy Hull, 'the unofficial mayor of the Shankill', was convenor of engineering union shop stewards in the engine shop at Harland and Wolff, and a member of his union's national appeals committee. Until August 1969 he had been a member of the Northern Ireland Labour party, resigning in protest at Wilson's intervention in Ulster's affairs. That same month he formed a Workers Committee for the Defence of the Constitution, as 'loyalist' as Paisley's UCDC but explicitly working-class in appeal and social composition. In the first issue of its short-lived publication

People's Press, it sounded a note of proletarian radicalism which at the time found few echoes in the wider 'loyalist' movement, but was to be revived a couple of years later:

The ordinary working people are the backbone of the United Kingdom, and this applies as much to Northern Ireland as to England, Scotland and Wales. The children of the workers deserve the opportunity of higher education, and statistics show that they are not getting it here today. Where there ought to be rows of terraced houses with modern bathrooms, up-to-date playing fields and old people's homes, swimming pools and normal necessities of life today, the Shankill Road and other workers' areas present a bleak picture of desolation . . . The leaders of Unionism have not inherited our automatic support.

It was, of course, 'loyalist' rather than social grievances which brought Billy Hull's men out against Chichester-Clark in March 1971. But the message was clear enough: the coalition of class interests which made up the Unionist Party was more than ever under threat. Chichester-Clark flew to London to press Heath to authorise internment, not because it was a military necessity but because his own survival, and that of official Unionism, depended on it. But the best Heath felt able to offer was an extra 1,300 troops. On 19 March Chichester-Clark resigned. Craig unsuccessfully challenged Faulkner for the leadership and a paragon of bourgeois values became the first Ulster politician to reach the top without benefit of a plantation pedigree. The *Protestant Telegraph* prophesied bitterly, but correctly, that Faulkner 'could be Ulster's shortest-reigning premier'.

At the end of March the Provisionals launched their bombing offensive. There were thirty-seven major explosions in April, forty-seven in May and fifty in June. One of Faulkner's first acts as prime minister was to persuade military intelligence and the RUC Special Branch to start drawing up lists of potential internees. Faulkner had a neat scheme. He would create a number of parliamentary committees and, in a flurry of reformism, offer paid chairmanships to the catholic opposition, now reorganised as the Social-Democratic and Labour Party. If they accepted, the IRA would be isolated. If they refused, their stubborn non-co-operation must surely change Westminster's mind on internment.

The SDLP accepted; but it was very soon clear that, far from leaving the IRA isolated, the party leaders had isolated themselves. They must needs perform a smart about-turn. The opportunity came on 7 July when the army shot two catholics dead in a street riot. The SDLP demanded a government inquiry, failing which they would not only turn down Faulkner's committee chairmanships but leave Stormont altogether to form an 'alternative assembly', as favoured by the IRA. Faulkner knew what commissions of inquiry could do to 'loyalist' morale, and he refused. Out of Stormont came the catholic opposition, never to return. Political institutions were beginning to crumble and with the July total of IRA bombings reaching ninety-one – three a day – Faulkner's arguments for internment began to get a hearing at Westminster.

On the last day of July there was a secret meeting in Belfast of Official IRA leaders and four leaders of the UVF. This was the only such meeting of which there is any record, and that only from IRA sources. The assumption was that internment had become inevitable and that Faulkner would demonstrate a studied impartiality by lifting at least a handful of protestant extremists. The meeting discussed what kinds of joint action might be undertaken to oppose arrests, and agreed in principle a 'united front' against the army and RUC should mass arrests begin. No statement was issued, both sides being unsure of the reaction of their respective followers to the bizarre alliance.

A not altogether dissimilar alliance was also apparent

in Stormont. Predictably, Paisley had been among the first to call for 'the implementation of the Special Powers Act against Republicans' back in September 1970, but by early 1971 he had begun to change his tune. His friend, ally, and increasingly his *eminence grise,* Desmond Boal, told Stormont on 27 January that internment should be opposed because the government was 'so stupid and so susceptible to outside, uninformed opinion, that they would want to intern 50 per cent protestants and 50 per cent Roman Catholics.' A month later Paisley took the same line, telling the Westminster parliament: 'Strange to say, I am opposed to internment . . . If the Northern Ireland government had the power of internment would be working on a 50-50 basis. They would say "We will put that man away because he is a Roman Catholic; we will put that man away because he is an Orangeman. He is a Free Presbyterian, so we will remove him as quickly as possible." '

When both Boal and Paisley stiffened up their opposition to a point at which they were able to join with the SDLP in declaring 'opposition in principle', they left behind them a number of confused followers. Among those who were quick to accuse Paisley of 'betrayal' were the leaders of the Shankill Defence Association, who had long been demanding internment in *Loyalist News.* The 'Crumlin Protestant Ladies Association', newly formed by Mrs Mina Browne, organised a pro-internment picket of MPs and followed this with an angry denunciation of Boal. Craig spoke cautiously of Paisley's 'miscalculation' and Brian Faulkner told friends that 'Paisley must have gone mad'. By July Paisley seemed on the point of switching back to his old line. 'Internment of all known IRA personnel would be a first step,' declared the *Protestant Telegraph,* adding that 'the vermin must be suppressed either by internment or effective action by our security forces'.

Early in August Faulkner secured the approval of the Westminster cabinet for the policy to which he now pinned all his hopes of ending violence and re-establishing protestant authority. At dawn on Monday 9 August troops lifted more than 300 men on their wanted lists. Arrests continued at the rate of eighty a week until more than 900 were interned. They included known IRA men, civil rights officials and socialist activists – but no 'loyalists'. The contingency plans agreed between the IRA and the UVF quickly lapsed as UVF leaders realised that they were to be left to continue their work undisturbed.

Within hours of the start of the army swoop, it began to be clear that, far from ending violence, internment had given the IRA its biggest boost since the troubles began. In three days of carnage it was estimated that 7,000 catholics and 2,000 protestants were forced to leave their homes, intimidated or burnt out. Two hundred houses were burnt by their fleeing protestant occupiers in an hysterical bid to stop them being taken over by rampaging catholics. The August bomb totals topped the 100 mark, and thirty-five people were killed – nearly twice as many as the total for the whole of 1970.

Suddenly Brian Faulkner's leadership was as insecure as ever O'Neill's and Chichester-Clark's had been. Contending now for the leadership of the 'loyalist' masses were Bill Craig and Ian Paisley, the one fighting inside, the other outside the ranks of the official Unionist Party.

At first their rivalry took the paradoxical form of an alliance. Craig, Paisley and Boal had several meetings in the three weeks following internment and on 4 September they announced the formation of a 'Unionist Alliance' between hard-liners in the Unionist Party and supporters of Paisley's Protestant Unionist and UCDC-UPV groups. The Alliance was chaired by Boal and joined by John McQuade, James Molyneaux MP (Sovereign Grand Master of the Royal Black Institution), Rev. Martin

Smyth (Orange County Grand Master, Belfast), two members of the UCDC and a dozen local Unionist officials. Its manifesto pledged members 'not only to protect our constitutional status but to restore its integrity ... using whatever non-violent means that changing circumstances may demand.' It was emphasised that 'the constituent groupings in the alliance will continue to hold their distinctive party affiliations.'

The Alliance was doomed from the start. Craig, who had a strong sense of the resilience of traditional Unionism linked with the Orange Order, hoped to harness the strength of 'loyalist' elements outside the party in his own bid for power. Paisley and Boal, on the other hand, saw the Alliance as the nucleus of a new party which would attract the disaffected protestant working class. Boal, in particular, saw the new party taking the opposition seats in Stormont vacated by the SDLP boycott. If and when the SDLP returned, the new party might join with them, on social if not on constitutional issues, as a non-sectarian working-class opposition.

When the Alliance was no more than a week old, Boal and McQuade announced their resignation from the Unionist Party. Craig reflected acidly that 'it was a pity, when Loyalists were beginning to get together, that people were resigning or dropping into a void.' And he gave the first, early indication of what was germinating in his own mind when he told an Ulster Hall rally on 28 September that 'it was time the constituency associations made a new move and provided a Unionist vanguard which would show the strength and capacity to create a new initiative in Unionism.'

The following night the Alliance was formally disbanded and Paisley made the first public announcement of a new party. Boal described the 'Democratic Unionist Party' as 'right-wing in the sense of being strong on the constitution and restoring security but to the left on social policies.' Success for the party depended on its

142

ability to provoke defections from the Unionists and it faced its first test on 3 October, when representatives of twenty-eight rebel Unionist Party constituency associations met in a Shankill Road hall to co-ordinate activities and discuss tactics. Paisley and Boal hoped that some, if not all, might be persuaded to declare for the DUP. But, while the delegates voted with predictable unanimity for Faulkner's resignation, they decided against breaking with official Unionism. Traditional ties were strong. Craig had won the first round.

But it was on the streets, and not behind closed doors, that the real battle for working-class 'loyalist' hearts and minds was being fought out, and to the streets we must now return.

In the summer of 1971, as the Provisional bombing campaign got under way, McKeague's SDA ran into factional disputes. On 8 May McKeague's shop and the flat above it were petrol-bombed and his elderly mother died in the blaze. Three protestants were arrested and held for twenty-two hours before being released. The *Loyalist News* pointedly refrained from blaming the IRA but described Mrs McKeague as having been 'murdered by the enemies of Ulster'.

In June, McKeague was prosecuted with two colleagues for publishing a *Loyalist Song Book* containing new and traditional 'kill the Taigs' songs which allegedly contravened the Prevention of Incitement to Race Hatred Act. But McKeague had the services of a good lawyer, Desmond Boal. The jury disagreed, and in a retrial all three defendants were acquitted.

Curiously, while the State was prepared to go into action against alleged incitement when it appeared in book form, it held its hand against McKeague's *Loyalist News* and a rival publication, the *Woodvale Defence Association Bulletin,* which were packed with much sterner material. Both papers carried frequent reference to the proscribed UVF, generally approving – except when the

UVF was rebuked for not being sufficiently militant, as in a letter in the *Loyalist News* on 3 July:

I want to remind protestants that these animals [the IRA] are crawling into Ulster, hitting vital points like RUC stations etc. The ugly thing is that the bastards are getting away with it. Then the question arises, What the hell is the UVF doing about it? You've got to fight fire with fire, and personally I don't think they've enough fire to make the animals sweat! I'm not against the UVF but I would like to see a new UVF fighting for the cause and willing to give their lives to hold on to what others gave their lives for.

What *was* the UVF doing? Gusty Spence was approaching the end of the fifth year of his twenty-year sentence in Crumlin Road jail. (The SDA organised a petition for his release in July 1971.) Outside, the UVF had almost ceased to exist as a co-ordinated force. Occasional acts of violence by *ad hoc* groups of militants were done in its name, and in the bars of the Shankill men made brave plans over their beer. But in July 1971 there was probably no more than a score of active UVF men, most of them long-time associates of Gusty Spence.

The explosion of catholic violence that followed internment in August was to change that. As homes burned and refugees fled, protestant vigilante groups sprang up everywhere. At the height of the violence, on 12 August, an anonymous leaflet was handed out on Shankill Road, Sandy Row and Ravenhill Road by a group of men, at least one of whom was to become prominent in the as yet unknown Ulster Defence Association. It read:

Being convinced that the enemies of the Faith and Freedom are determined to destroy the State of Northern Ireland and thereby enslave the people of God, we call on all members of our loyalist institutions, and other responsible citizens, to organise themselves *immediately* into Platoons of twenty under the command of someone capable of acting as Sergeant. Every effort must be made to arm these Platoons with whatever weapons are available. The first duty of each Platoon will be to formulate a plan for the defence of its own street or road in co-operation with Platoons in adjoining areas. A structure of Command is already in existence and the various Platoons will eventually be linked in a co-ordinated effort.

Instructions: Under no circumstances must Platoons come into conflict with Her Majesty's Forces or the Police. If through wrong Political direction Her Majesty's Forces are directed against loyalist people members of Platoons must do everything possible to prevent a confrontation. We are loyalists, we are Queen's men! Our enemies are the forces of Romanism and Communism which must be destroyed.

Members of Platoons must act with the highest sense of responsibility and urgency in preparing our people for the full assault of the enemies within our Province and the forces of the Eire Government which will eventually be thrown against us. We must prepare now! This is total war!

At the same time a crudely stencilled poster went up in protestant areas of East Belfast: 'Join the 2nd East Belfast Battalion UVF.'

By the end of August there were vigilante groups or 'defence associations' or 'platoons' in Shankill, Woodvale, Ormeau, Carrick, Donegall Pass, Hammer, Newtownabbey, Abbots Cross, Woodburn, Lisburn Road, Seymour Hill, Suffolk, Castlereagh, Beersbridge, Upper Woodstock and Dundonald. Early in September, Charles Harding Smith, a founder-member of Woodvale Defence Association, took the initiative in bringing them all together under a central council, the Ulster Defence Association. The UDA adopted an incongruous Latin motto, *Cedenta Arma Togae,* law before violence, and declared that its aim was 'to see law restored everywhere, including the no-go areas'. Rather pointedly it stipulated that 'no MPs and no religious mentors' would be admitted to membership. Vigilantes were urged to style themselves 'Ulster Volunteers'.

Inevitably the UVF felt that others were muscling in on

their territory and a determined bid was made to take over the more important constituent associations in the UDA. The new *UDA Bulletin* had occasion to warn its readers:

Extremist groups have been surprised by the growth of the UDA. They know it poses a threat to their existence. These extremist groups put themselves first and the UDA second and Ulster a very poor third. At the moment these extremists are trying to take over the local defence groups. Don't let them. Already they have tried to involve the UDA in unjustified discrimination. We know who we will discriminate against, and this includes protestants whose only interest is their own interests.

The UDA 'volunteers' were the most dramatic product of post-internment violence but there was another of equal importance. In Harland's shipyard and Short's missile and armoured car plant, Billy Hull revived his Workers' Committee for the Defence of the Constitution and re-constituted it as the Loyalist Association of Workers – LAW. Branches were opened at the giant Mackie's foundry and Gallaher's tobacco factory, and the strength of organised working-class 'loyalism' was demonstrated on 6 September when 25,000 workers downed tools for an afternoon rally in Victoria Park chaired by Hull and addressed by Craig and Paisley. Hull announced that 'the age of the rubber bullet is over. It's lead bullets from now on . . . We are British to the core but we won't hesitate to take on even the British if they attempt to sell our country down the river'.

It was against this background of mounting grass-roots militancy that Boal, Paisley and Craig fought out their battle for the leadership of Ulster loyalism. If Craig could win the UDA militants and the LAW mass base, his chances of taking over the Unionist Party from within, and preserving the traditional pattern of class collaboration, were enormously enhanced. If the DUP could win their allegiance, the protestant working class would make an historic break with Unionism and change the face of Ulster politics.

Craig saw what was at stake and made his pitch accordingly. But Paisley's eyes were on another prize. Following Boal's grand strategy for a united opposition to official Unionism, Paisley met the SDLP leaders secretly late in October. According to an account of the meeting leaked to a Dublin journalist, the DUP and SDLP agreed to differ on the constitution but found themselves in agreement on internment, opposition to 'community government' (fixed quotas of protestants and catholics in Stormont committees), and the need for an urgent drive against unemployment by massive state intervention and public works. No pacts were made, no agreements signed. But the far-reaching implications of the meeting were clear. 'Wolfe Tone,' commented one of the SDLP members, 'is alive and well and leading the Democratic Unionist Party.'

There was more confusion among Paisley's supporters when, at a meeting on 30 October, he claimed to have it from 'a very good authority and source at Westminster' that direct rule was imminent. It was not the prediction but Paisley's reaction to it which was confusing. 'Those of us who favour the British connection,' he said, 'will at least see in this that we will be more integrated than ever in the United Kingdom.' From one who had long threatened the direst consequences should Stormont be tampered with, this was a strange turn of the cheek. Certainly it gave Paisley a better claim to moderation than Faulkner, who ridiculed the prediction but also took the precaution to threaten a 'violent holocaust' should Westminster try it on.

A few days later the new Paisleyism surfaced again when Boal attacked the most sacred of Unionism's sacred cows, the link with the Orange Order. 'How can we complain about the sinister influence of the Roman Catholic

Church in the political and social life of the Republic,' he asked, 'when we ourselves are vulnerable to the charge that direct representation of the Orange Order in the government party may arouse in Roman Catholics a corresponding fear that what is to them just as malign an influence exists in the bodies that decide policy in this country?'

On 25 November Harold Wilson published his 15-point plan for an Irish settlement, and the DUP made another lurch towards liberalism. That night Paisley and Boal agreed to meet three Dublin journalists to pronounce on the Wilson plan. Henry Kelly of the *Irish Times*, Vincent Browne of the *Irish Press* and Liam Hourican of Radio Telefis Eireann found their hosts prepared to go further than any of their 'moderate' opponents in examining the ultimate unity of Ireland. The principal obstacle to unity, said Paisley in a radio interview, was the Republic's theocratic constitution, and if this were changed 'you would have an entirely different set of circumstances'. In his *Irish Times* interview he was a little more specific. If protestants could be sure that the catholic church could no longer dictate policy to the Dublin government, that home rule no longer meant Rome rule, 'then there would be a new set of circumstances, where there could be good neighbourliness in the highest possible sense, and in those circumstances there would be a situation different from any that existed when the country was divided.' Asked whether he could see 'some time, some way, somewhere in the future a united Ireland,' he replied: 'That is a question I cannot answer because I cannot now say what will happen in the future.'

Suddenly Paisley was a celebrity, a hero, in the Republic. Finance Minister George Colley invited him to Dublin to help draft a new constitution, and David O'Connell of the Provisional IRA high command described Republicans and Democratic Unionists as 'allies in the cause of a New Ireland'. Sean Cronin the veteran Republican who

148

had led the IRA border campaign in the 1950s, wrote that 'without a doubt a "New Ireland" of some kind is struggling towards birth. And one of the midwives will be Ian Paisley . . .'

The men and women for whom Paisley speaks are of the same stock as the people who brought democracy to Ireland, and, in the process, republicanism. Paisley's vaguely populist political philosophy has overtones of traditional republicanism. There are wide differences in views, of course, but both sides can stand on more common ground than most people realise.

Watching the at first bemused and then enraged reactions of their followers to all this, Paisley and Boal realised that they had gone too far. Faulkner, seizing his opportunity, dubbed Paisley 'the darling of the Republican press, wooed by Messrs. Colley and Lynch'. McKeague's *Loyalist News* jubilantly shrieked 'betrayal!' The *UDA Bulletin,* noting that 'at one time we would have followed Paisley anywhere,' went on to offer 'thanks for his original efforts in forging Loyalists together' – and bade him goodbye. Paisley was on his own.

He began to backtrack fast. He was 'opposed absolutely' to any kind of united Ireland, he told a BBC interviewer on 9 December. He had been misreported, misquoted, misunderstood. In a desperate bid to re-establish credit with those of his followers whose interpretation of fundamental loyalism was less flexible than his own, he reverted to the old, discredited tactic of threatening a new wave of counter-demonstrations against civil rights marches. His UPV divisions, which had not been heard of for a year or more, issued a statement accusing the government of having 'neither the wish nor the will to resist Popish encroachment'. The statement ended: 'All True Blue Loyalists have always answered Ulster's cause. Ulster will fight and Ulster will be right! No surrender!' It was back to 1968 (or 1912, or 1690) with a vengeance.

And it was unavailing. The massed ranks of the UDA were looking elsewhere for leadership, and William Craig was looking for followers. Paisley, whose rhetoric had given birth to the new protestant Volunteer movement, saw it stolen from under his nose just as it threatened to take off as a mass movement. The protestant working class was back under the frayed but familiar skirts of official Unionism.

10   REALIGNMENTS

The start of 1972 saw Ulster waiting with tense expectation for the British government's package deal. Any lingering hopes that the two warring communities might yet be reconciled were smashed in Londonderry on 30 January when troops of the 2nd Parachute Regiment shot thirteen civil rights demonstrators dead. Catholics talked of 'Bloody Sunday' but John McKeague went on television to say that 'loyalists' called it 'Good Sunday' and were only sorry that more IRA scum had not got what they clearly deserved.

But the trigger-happy paratroopers had executed sentence of death on traditional British policy in Northern Ireland. Bloody Sunday, following as it did the shock report of Sir Edmund Compton revealing extensive and systematic 'ill treatment' of internees, emphasised the consequences of committing British security forces to the support of Stormont. A new 'initiative' was now inevitable, and Unionist politicians braced themselves for the worst.

In the week following Bloody Sunday, William Craig launched the movement he had first hinted at back in September: Ulster Vanguard. It was, he said, 'an association of associations', an umbrella movement for traditional 'loyalist' groupings. Under the umbrella came half the Unionist constituency parties, the Orange Order (at least in Belfast), the Apprentice Boys, Billy Hull's Loyalist Association of Workers, the 20,000-strong Ulster Special Constabulary Association and some, but not all, of the street vigilante organisations of the UDA. Vanguard immediately embarked on a series of weekend rallies from 12 February to what was expected to be Stormont's Easter recess at the end of March.

The first was at Lisburn. By Ulster standards it was not large, but it struck a sinister note. Craig, arriving with an impressive motor-cycle escort, walked up and down silent lines of some six hundred men, drawn up in military formation. Announced simply as 'the leader', he proceeded to read a long 'Declaration of Intent and Covenant to Act', clearly modelled on the 1912 covenant of the UVF, asking all those who assented to raise their hands three times and say 'I do'. The serried ranks responded with arms upraised and gullets at full throttle and millions who saw the event on television found themselves watching an action replay of the rallies of the Third Reich. 'We are determined, ladies and gentlemen, to preserve our British traditions and way of life,' Craig concluded. 'And God help those who get in our way.'

Such sentiments were well calculated to appeal to the growing numbers involved in the 'Volunteer forces' on the streets, whose proliferating news-sheets vividly expressed the frustrations of men and women who lacked only a recognised leader and a commonly agreed course of action. The following letter to the *UDA Bulletin* from a woman reader was by no means untypical:

I have reached the stage where I no longer have any compassion for any Nationalist, man, woman or child. After years of destruction, murder, intimidation, I have been driven against my better feelings to the decision – it's them or us. What I want to know is this, where the hell are MEN in our community. Have they any pride? Have they any guts? Why are they not organised in, not defence, but commando groups? Why have they not started to hit back in the only way these Nationalist bastards understand? That is ruthless, indiscriminate killing . . . If I had a flame-thrower I would roast the slimy excreta that pass for human beings. Also I'm sick and tired of you yellow-backed Prods who are not even prepared to fight for your own street, let alone your own loyalist people. When civil war breaks out, and God forgive me, but I hope it's soon, I, at least, will shoot you along with the Fenian scum.

To which the editor replied: 'Without question most protestants would agree with your sentiments. We do. The greatest contribution that you can make to the destruction of the murderous Provos, IRA and Nationalists is to direct your energies into the UDA.'

But the UDA was rent by murderous rivalries. One faction fighting for control was based on McKeague's Shankill Defence Association, another on the Woodvale Defence Association led by Charles Harding Smith, and yet another on the UVF. Each faction was busily building up its own armoury, and the UVF pulled off the most spectacular coup by arranging the purchase of £600-worth of rifles, sub-machine guns and ammunition from Private Mervyn Hall, a twenty-year-old soldier in the Parachute Regiment. Hall was court-martialled and sentenced (without publicity) to two years, but his clients and their hardware were never traced.

Against this background, Craig's Ulster Vanguard made its bid for the UDA's support. McKeague was one of the first to offer the hand of friendship (though Craig was soon to find the fist clenched), his *Loyalist News* proclaiming: 'What Ulster needs today is a LEADER . . . The man we believe can do it is William Craig.' But *The Warrior,* organ of a rival East Belfast group, disagreed:

To win the civil war, what do we need? The first and inevitable point is the removal of the British army. To do this we need a strong organisation. Does Vanguard fulfil the requirements of a strong organisation? Unfortunately the answer is No. Why? Because what we need is a military organisation with all that this implies, including a military commander. Craig does not fit the bill.

The UDA's own *Bulletin* at first took the anti-Vanguard line. 'Why,' it asked early in February, 'has Craig formed another "loyalist" association? To build an organisation on personalities is to build it upon sand.' But on 8 February the UDA leadership was reorganised at a secret meeting in Antrim. The anonymous council which emerged from that meeting met for the first time on 15 February and one of its first decisions was to pledge 'full support' for Vanguard. When the editor of the *UDA Bulletin* showed some reluctance to toe the new line he was beaten up and deposed – but not before he had time to describe the attack in his last issue. The next issue of the paper carried an announcement that it was now under the control of the central council, which had removed the former editor for 'misrepresenting the movement' and allegedly pocketing the proceeds from the paper's sales. Thereafter, for a time, there was no more criticism of Vanguard from official UDA sources and the UDA assumed, for a time, the role of Vanguard's paramilitary wing.

Craig's rhetoric became increasingly violent. On 5 March, in an RTE television interview, he talked of the action that 'loyalists' might feel compelled to take against those they considered the enemies of Ulster. 'Would this mean killing all catholics in Belfast?' he was asked. 'It might not go so far as that,' Craig conceded, 'but it could go as far as killing.' There was no word of rebuke for these remarks from Faulkner, who saw Vanguard and the UDA as a trump card to play with Westminster. Only Desmond Boal clearly pointed out where such talk led. 'People who were fearful or frustrated,' he said, 'were usually a prey to the suggestion that force was the only solution. If not given specific targets, people would find their own targets and that would mean that innocent Roman Catholics would suffer.' Random sectarian assassination, in other words, as in the Malvern Street murder.

And by early March there was evidence that organised activity along these lines had already begun. In the last week of February a catholic was shot dead from a passing

154

car on the Springfield Road. Another was killed in the same fashion in Lurgan and a third, a woman, in Durham Street, Belfast, shot from a car which sped off towards Sandy Row. In Newry a catholic youth had the letters UVF carved on his stomach with broken glass, an experience which Austin Currie's wife was to share later in the year. The father of an internee was shot from a passing car on the edge of the catholic Short Strand area of East Belfast, and a catholic youth was wounded in similar circumstances in the Markets area. On 21 March a Provisional Sinn Fein meeting was attacked by machine-gun fire in Emyvale, county Monaghan, the fire again being directed from a passing car which sped off across the border into Northern Ireland. SDLP MPs Paddy Devlin and Ivan Cooper both reported attempts on their lives, one by gunfire from a car and one by a bomb blast. Later, in the five days between 15 April and 20 April, three more catholics were shot dead from passing cars, apparently at random, and another two seriously wounded.

As in 1966, Belfast newspaper offices began to receive messages signed by the UVF. One such letter to the *Newsletter* on 8 March warned that ten men, including a catholic priest, would be shot for every member of the security forces killed. It claimed that the UVF was ready to go into action and 'if the order to kill was given, it would take the enemies of the state two months to bury their dead'. The police, to whom the letter was handed, chose to regard it as a hoax. Three days later the Rev. William McCrea, minister of Magherafelt Free Presbyterian Church, publicly called for the ban on the UVF to be lifted so that its members could openly 'aid the security forces'.

With so marked an escalation of protestant violence, it was inevitable that some of the bomb explosions hitherto attributed to the IRA would now be put down to 'loyalist' extremism. On 4 March a bomb in the Abercorn Restaurant, Belfast, killed two and injured 136, many critically. The usual IRA warnings were not given in this instance, and both wings denied responsibility. Provisional Sinn Féin then accused the protestants, alleging that the Abercorn had been threatened in the Woodvale Defence Association's news-sheet. The WDA denied ever having made any reference to the Abercorn, and Sinn Féin were unable to make the charge stick.

They were, nevertheless, on the right track. Not the WDA news-sheet but *UDA News*, issue no. 12 undated but published in January, had carried a story to the effect that a group of protestants in the Abercorn had been prevented by the management from singing the British national anthem at their Christmas party. The implication was that the restaurant was run by 'rebels'. But the affiliation of the unknown bombers was never proved. It is by no means impossible that this particularly mindless act was the work of a protestant gang, but it could equally have been committed by the 'UVF Unit' newly formed by the Provisional IRA to divert attention from its own campaign. The unit is known to have been organised at the beginning of the year and to have bombed a number of empty catholic-owned public houses to create the illusion of a real UVF bombing campaign.

A new Westminster initiative was now imperative, and as speculation mounted on the form it would take, Craig held his biggest Vanguard rally to date in Belfast's Ormeau Park on 18 March. Some 60,000 attended, including several thousand masked and uniformed men and 2,000 former B Specials. Craig promised the formation of a 'provisional government' should Westminster attempt to force through a new constitution against the will of the majority, and he went on: 'We must build up the dossier on those men and women in this country who are a menace to this country, because one of these days, if and when the politicians fail us, it may be our job to liquidate the enemy.'

Ian Paisley picked up this chilling reference and made

it the text of a scathing attack on Vanguard. He exposed the patent contradiction between Vanguard's UDI aspirations and its professions of traditional Unionism, and finally stated flatly that in his view it would be better to integrate Ulster fully into the United Kingdom rather than tinker with a Stormont which had clearly failed the Ulster people. For Paisley, full integration now seemed a treble blessing. It would preserve the Union, kill off the Unionist Party, and leave himself, alone among all the 'loyalist' leaders, with a continuing platform in Westminster.

At 11 a.m. on 24 March, Edward Heath called Vanguard's bluff. Stormont, he announced, was to be suspended for a year and Northern Ireland ruled by a Secretary of State responsible to Westminster. Fifty years of Tory misrule were abruptly ended by a Tory prime minister.

It was the moment of truth for Vanguard, the UDA and the UVF. At secret meetings throughout Ulster there were passionate and bitter arguments over whether or not the 'loyalist' organisations should put their trigger fingers where their mouths were and declare war on the British. At one meeting in Belfast, Jock Beckett, an executive member of the Loyalist Association of Workers, attacked a particularly militant faction as 'not men at all, only a bunch of thugs and gangsters'. That night he was shot dead and his body dumped in a side street off Shankill Road. His sister, Mrs Jean Moore, who was later to run the women's section of the UDA, accused a UDA faction of killing him.

But it was to Vanguard that all eyes were turned. Its 'Declaration of Intent and Covenant to Act' had pledged the movement to 'take whatsoever action we consider best' to preserve 'strong, effective, undiluted majority rule in Ulster'. Strong, effective, undiluted majority rule was precisely what the prorogation of Stormont prevented. What action, then, would Vanguard consider best?

Craig gave his answer on 26 March: a two-day 'loyalist'

strike, another rally (shared with Faulkner) and a boycott of goods from the Republic. 'Vanguard feels its cause will best be served by peaceful pressure,' explained Craig limply. The promised 'provisional government' was forgotten, replaced by nothing more muscular than a boycott of Kerrygold butter.

Had the protestant threat to fight always been an empty pretence, from Randolph Churchill and Carson to Paisley in the 1960s and Vanguard in 1972? The truth is that, whatever the real strength of their resolution, 'loyalists' had never cleared their minds on *when* they would fight and against whom. Vanguard had sharpened up the militancy without cutting through the old confusions. Craig and Billy Hull and the UDA leaders never sorted out in their own minds whether it was to be an enforced reform programme, the suspension or diminution or abolition of Stormont, a federal constitution or the wholesale abandonment of the north to a 32-county republic which would cause them to let loose the protestant dogs of war. Nor had they cleared their minds on whom they would be fighting: the IRA, the Irish army or the soldiers of the Queen in whose name they would presumably be firing their guns. 24 March 1972 consequently found Vanguard an impotent Gargantua.

The one protestant leader who, by 1972, had done something to cut through these confusions was Paisley. Despite what he had said in his UCDC constitution back in 1966, Armageddon was not to be invoked against reforms: indeed, Paisley himself had now turned reformer. Nor against the suspension of Stormont, which damaged only the dignity of corrupt Unionists. Nor against a federal arrangement which might yet reconcile 'good neighbourliness' towards the Republic with the British link. Ulster would fight, promised Paisley, if Ulster were coerced into a sectarian Dublin parliament. Only this ultimate betrayal would push a million protestants into violent insurrection.

Vanguard continued its huffing and puffing, carrying its

protests to the new seat of power, London, on 29 April, where its rally was supported and serviced by the extreme right-wing National Front. But seemingly much more sinister was a private meeting that evening in London's Hilton Hotel, resulting in five arrests over an alleged massive £350,000 arms plot. The arrested men included Charles Harding Smith, the UDA chairman, and he was to remain in custody for nearly eight months until finally released on acquittal the following December.

According to the prosecution at their Old Bailey trial, Smith and his associates were negotiating the illegal purchase of a consignment of rifles worth £100,000, and more modern weapons worth £250,000. Charged with Smith was a former B Special, John Campbell, director of a Belfast firm of firearms dealers, 'Guns and Tackle'. Campbell's licence to deal in prohibited weapons such as sub-machineguns and assault rifles was revoked on Home Office authority in August 1969, leaving him able to deal only in revolver, shotguns and rifles. Three other men, John White, Robert Dalzell and an RUC officer named Robert Lusty, referred to in court as 'Mr Z', were also accused.

The story that unfolded in court rivalled a James Bond screenplay. In February 1972 Campbell phoned a gun holster manufacturer named as 'Witness A' and told him he had £50,000 to spend, but not on holsters. 'A' understood him to be referring to prohibited weapons, and put him in touch with a Scottish arms supplier called 'B'. Campbell arranged to meet 'B' in a West End pub and took two men with him. One was Smith, the other the RUC man, 'Z'. According to the prosecution, Campbell said the protestants had 'had their noses rubbed in it for two or three years and were not going to take any more'. He asked 'B' to supply him with assault rifles and sub-machineguns, telling him that money was limitless and that there was at least £100,000 available. He said he had already bought £100,000-worth that Easter. Campbell described 'Z' as his bodyguard and said Smith was there 'to help carry the cash'. But 'B' said he could not conclude a deal without consulting his principals.

A second meeting was arranged for 29 April at the Hilton. This one was less private. 'B', it turned out, was a Lanarkshire special constable named William Sinclair and his 'principal' was a Special Branch officer, Sgt Michael Waller. Plain-clothes detectives watched and listened as Campbell, accompanied by Dalzell, White and 'Z', met 'B' and his secret Special Branch contact and again solicited the supply of assault rifles to the value of £100,000. According to the prosecution, Campbell said he would take whatever 'B' could supply and he would place a further order for more modern equipment in the region of a quarter of a million pounds. The next order, he promised, would be 'government to government', which his listeners understood as a reference to an independent protestant government of Ulster.

Then, at a given signal, the plain-clothes detectives revealed themselves and the four men were arrested. Later, Smith called at Scotland Yard and said he knew the four men, but refused to answer further questions. He was then arrested himself, whereupon he told the police: 'Before you go any further, contact the British army in Belfast. I have saved lives. I am in charge of the Ulster Defence Association in Belfast.' A search of his home was ordered and police found intelligence reports on IRA personnel, gathered by what was described in court as a 'secret army'. Smith agreed that he had a classified list of men recently released from internment and said he knew he should not have had it.

'Z' was discharged at an early stage of the trial. White and Dalzell claimed they were only drinking at the Hilton and knew nothing of an arms plot. But Smith and Campbell did not deny the substance of the court's story. They claimed, however, that at both meetings they had been trying to trap suspected IRA gun-runners. Campbell said he had thought that 'B' might be supplying the IRA and he had arranged the bogus negotiations in the hope of finding the source of IRA weapons. Smith produced a character reference from the RUC Chief Constable, saying he had assisted the security forces in Northern Ireland. All the defendants were acquitted by jury of incitement to deal in prohibited weapons and six related charges. On 20 December Smith returned to Belfast to rejoin a UDA which, in his absence, had grown to a strength of 60,000 and had overtaken the IRA as the Northern Ireland administration's biggest headache. On 10 January 1973 he was reinstated as joint chairman.

But back in May, with Smith in custody and likely to remain there for some time, the UDA was forced to undergo a further reshuffle at the top. There was more in-fighting in which John McKeague, who had turned to criticising Craig's leadership of Vanguard, was forced out of the movement altogether, only to form a secret paramilitary group of his own, the Red Hand Commandos, about whose activities one can only speculate. The new UDA chairman was Jim Anderson, a forty-two-year-old glazier, who took the rank of 'Major-General' as the movement reorganised itself on straight military lines. His vice-chairman and 'Brigadier' was a thirty-four-year-old garage manager, Tommy Herron, who soon emerged as the movement's public spokesman. Beneath them were eleven 'Colonels' or 'Lieutenant-Colonels', together making a 13-man Inner Council whose identities were successfully kept secret for many months. They were Samuel Doyle (Oldpark and Crumlin districts), David Fogel, a Londoner and ex-army NCO (Woodvale and Ardoyne), John Graham, a former SDA man (Shankill), Ernest Willis (Rathcoole), Tom McCreary (Ballysillan), Billy Rowan, an old associate of Major Bunting (half of Newtownards and Dundonald), Frank Jones (Woodstock and Cregagh), Edward McCreery (half of Newtownards), Jack Watson (Sandy Row and Lisburn Road), 'Duke' Ernie Elliott (second in command, Woodvale), and David Payne (second in command, Shankill).

The new leadership came up with a tough new policy, the avowed aim of which was to force the British army to invade and end the catholic no-go areas, 'failing which we'll do the job ourselves'. For five successive weekends, starting on 13 May, the UDA would set up its own token no-go areas in protestant parts of Belfast. If at the end of that period the catholic enclaves had still not been tackled, the 'loyalist' areas of Belfast and Londonderry would be 'permanently' closed to troops and police.

On 13 May the Woodvale area was barricaded by improvised road blocks and hijacked buses. Manning the barricades were several hundred UDA men in the combat jackets and hoods which were to become so depressingly familiar a part of the Ulster scene in the coming months. The men stood in ranks for the benefit of press photographers, looking for all the world the mirror-image of IRA vigilantes in the Bogside – which was precisely the impression they intended to convey. The headlines next morning were heavy with 'backlash', a word that began to look an understatement when, that same weekend, six men and a child were killed in three-way gun battles between catholics in Ballymurphy, protestants in Springmartin and troops in between. As both communities buried their dead later in the week, the protestants as well as the catholics chose IRA-type military funerals, scores of marching protestants wearing for the first time replicas of the old UVF badge.

The weekend barricades went up again on 20 May, this time in parts of East Belfast and the Shankill. The army tried to talk them down, failed, and moved in with bulldozers. They were met with stones, bottles and eventually gunfire, and they returned gunfire and CS gas. A UDA spokesman was reported as saying: 'I'm beginning to think those people in the Bogside were right about Bloody Sunday. The paratroops behave madly.'

The UDA's new militancy embarrassed Craig, who declared that Vanguard was 'not in principle in favour of no-go areas'. But the weekend barricade-building continued. On 3 June a fifty-strong UVF contingent helped establish a no-go area in Londonderry and McKeague's Red Hand Commandos established one in Bangor. Frightened that he was losing whatever control he thought he had over the militants, Craig fielded a new paramilitary body on 10 June, a 500-strong Orange Volunteer force of ex-servicemen organised under the direct control of Vanguard. Those, along with a 200-strong 'Vanguard service corps' formed to steward Craig's rallies, and some 12,000 members of the Special Constabulary Association, made up 'Ulster Guard', Vanguard's own commando force independent of the UDA. But the UDA remained nominally under Vanguard's umbrella through its close association with LAW.

The army decided against repeating its attempt to bulldoze away the weekend no-go areas, but relations between them and the UDA continued to worsen. Woodvale's *WDA News* described an incident in which a plain-clothes army patrol, chasing four UDA men in a car, was surrounded by a 'loyalist' crowd, beaten up and their car set on fire.

The things that happened after the Special Branch creeps were stopped should be a grave warning to all loyalists. A briefcase was lifted from their car, and when searched was found to contain a number of match boxes containing bullets, nylon stockings cut and made into masks, magazines and photographs of an incriminating nature. The only reason that such a strange consignment could be in the car seems to be that they were to be used to implicate loyalists and for blackmail. We appeal to you, the loyalist people, to be on your guard against these scum.

With the deadline for permanent no-go areas drawing nearer, Secretary of State William Whitelaw stepped in with a private appeal to the UDA to defer their threatened doomsday. He could point to some successes in the war with the IRA. The Officials had announced a 'suspension of offensive operations' at the end of May. The Provisionals were under pressure to do the same, and did so, briefly, at the end of June. Flattered by Whitelaw's personal attention, the UDA council agreed to postpone its coup. But when Whitelaw once again made it plain that he was not yet prepared to sanction a military invasion of the Bogside and the Falls, the plan was revived. On 30 June, concrete blocks and iron stakes set into the road marked the establishment of 'permanent' protestant no-go areas.

And that same Saturday afternoon, Gusty Spence appeared on the Shankill, for the first time since Peter Ward was murdered six years before, almost to the day.

He had been given two days parole to attend the wedding of his daughter, Elizabeth – and here he was, inspecting the new barricades. For months Spence had been the Shankill's absent folk-hero, the man who, long before his fellows, had seen what the IRA was up to and had known how to stop them. He was idolised for the deed of which he had been convicted, and simultaneously hailed as an innocent victim of a political show-trial stage-managed by the traitor O'Neill. His name was on every gable wall in the Shankill and nowhere in larger letters than on the wall of the Malvern Arms, pock-marked with the bullet holes of 25 June 1966.

Yet barely nine months earlier, Spence had been described bitterly as 'Ulster's forgotten man' by some of his friends. They had watched as, through the autumn of 1971, the catholic community had rallied behind 'the men behind the wire', and they had decided it was high time they ran a campaign for the release of Spence and forty other protestant prisoners 'whose only crime was loyalty'.

The result was 'Orange Cross', formed at the end of 1971. Its secretary was Edward Spence, Gusty's nephew, son of the dominant personality in the Spence family,

William. It ran a weekend bookstall on the Shankill Road and, from February 1972 on, published a monthly paper, *Orange Cross,* 'Voice of the Loyalist Political Prisoners', largely written inside Crumlin Road jail. The first issue contained the following rationale of 'loyalist' extremism:

In Crumlin Road jail languish over 40 Loyalists. Unmourned by 99 per cent of Loyalists . . . Some are guilty of criminal (?) acts, some of political acts which were defined by the judge as criminal undoubtedly on instructions from higher authority. But we, the Loyalists, must remember that these acts were carried out by men in defending not only themselves but their friends and neighbours . . .
Ah! But they are extremists!
If you and your friends and your neighbours are being subject to unprovoked assault; when they are being subject to bombs, bullets, murder and arson; when the army and police refuse to police the areas from whence these outrages are being perpetrated, then what would you do? We can't all be rational under stress. Under normal circumstances these pent-up emotions within us are released by the forces of law and order taking legal action. But when such forces are ineffective in carrying out their duty, then the ordinary citizen must take action to protect himself from present and future attack. This is what these imprisoned Loyalists did. How can we, the rest of the ordinary citizens, condemn them for what we ourselves might have done under similar circumstances?

Orange Cross made it clear that the upsurge of 'loyalist' militancy on the streets was reflected within the prison walls. It reported the formation in February of a 'UVF Club' in the jail, with Spence as commanding officer. Other UVF clubs were being formed outside, said the paper, the first being a 'Rocky Burns UVF Club' in Lisburn (of which, however, nothing more was heard). *Orange Cross* and other 'loyalist' papers carried messages, philosophical and exhortatory, from Spence's own pen. One thanked the bookstall organisers for their support, which he interpreted as 'a mandate of sanction for the actions we took as free men, and as an act of solidarity with our aims in any further actions that we may take'. Another, in the name of the 'Joint Command', urged supporters: 'Stand back and have a good look at what is happening to our country, and be never more determined that the Republican scourge shall be eradicated and eliminated from the face of our fair land.'

Spence was also a poet – of sorts. This, for instance, on 'An Extremist':

When Ulster is in danger the Extremists will take a hand
Because they have an extreme love for their native land,
A Faith, a Crown and a way of life they will never sacrifice,
But will fight like Loyal Ulstermen, not timid Ulstermice.

And this, titled 'Prediction', which seems to relate to the events of 1966:

Pay attention you Informers to what I relate
And you will have an inkling of what will be your fate.
You betrayed a comrade's trust – the future you hold in dread.
Some night, some place, you will see a strange face
And he will shoot you dead.

Or this, called 'A Coward':

Accepted by us all as a man both staunch and true
When he swore a secret oath to stand by me and you,
He knew our cause was just, our actions stern inspired.
Little did we know – he was a coward.

He lost all sense of loyalty, informed upon his clan,
Can we truly and sincerely class this object as a man? . . .
For this wretch will surely die, from a bullet duly fired
By one he has betrayed – he was a coward.

This was the public Gusty Spence, obligingly conforming to the image projected by those who fostered his personality cult. But there was another Spence, a much more private Spence of which there had never been a hint before 1966 when a lonely cell first served to concentrate his wild mind.

As with so many 'political' prisoners before him, he found prison a university. It gave him opportunities to reflect and to read. Above all, it forced him into intimate contact with the men he professed to hate above all others: men of the IRA. Living, eating, exercising, socialising with them, he made the deeply unsettling discovery that many were men very much like himself: working men, born and bred to ghetto life, despising the soft middle class, and fired by fanatical enthusiasm for the patriot game. He began to make friends, not with Provisionals, who tended to keep to themselves, but with Officials whose consciously class-orientated, socialist philosophy made them anxious to extend a comradely hand. An Official IRA volunteer named Michael Willis became a particular friend, and once Spence had begun to articulate a rudimentary social programme – something that had never before concerned the UVF – he found it not very different from that of the Official IRA.

While nothing of this gradual metamorphosis is apparent in the messages and communiqués addressed to his Shankill Road followers, hints of it break through in an extraordinary collection of tapes secretly recorded in his cell and smuggled out to his family. Here Spence seems to be thinking aloud, now commenting on some domestic matter, now breaking into great chunks of his favourite poet, Kipling, now reminiscing about his Cyprus demonstration with Paisley or invoking the memory of Thomas McDowell, the UVF man killed in the 1966 Ballyshannon explosion, and now venting a new hatred: not of Republicanism but of Unionism. He reflects bitterly on 'fifty years of Tory misrule', on the way in which the 'loyalist' working class has been swindled, on the scandal of housing conditions in the Shankill, on the 'fraudulent suggestion' that protestant workers were part of an 'ascendancy'.

On 15 April an event occurred which led to Spence putting something of his new persona firmly on record. In the Markets area of Belfast, Official IRA leader Joe McCann was shot dead in the street by a British army marksman. McCann was to catholic Belfast what Spence was on the Shankill. He had once done Spence a favour, apparently ordering the release of two captured UVF men. Two days after his death, Spence wrote the following extraordinary letter to his widow:

My Dear Mrs McCann, I would like to tender to you my deepest and profoundest sympathy on the tragic death of your beloved Husband, Joe.

There are those who would find it strange to hear from someone such as myself but I can assure you that whilst your Husband and I may have been opposed to each other in Politics we shared that common bond that is known only to those who fight their own respective corners to the best of their ability. He was a soldier of the Republic and I a Volunteer of Ulster and we made no apology for being what we are or were.

Joe once did me a good turn indirectly and I never forgot him for his humanity and even though I never got the chance to thank him personally I am almost sure that he knew how I felt and that I was grateful to him.

In such circumstances, my inept words are little comfort to you but if you believe that these words are from the bottom of my heart it may go some little way to enabling you to understand them.

I, too, am a Family man with a Wife and four lovely Children and this aspect is the most heart-rending of all because the Women suffer in our coming and in our going and it is they who have the most courage.

May God bless your 'wee' ones and yourself in your hour of extreme grief and may He give you the strength required to face the future as Joe would have wished it.

I salute your Husband as an honourable and brave Soldier. Very Sincerely and Truly, Gusty Spence.

It was almost certainly the trauma of McCann's death which led Spence, a few days later, to take the unprecedented step of publicly associating the 'loyalist' prisoners with an IRA campaign. Thirty Official IRA prisoners were pressing for political status. Spence and thirty-four protestant prisoners publicly proclaiming their allegiance to the UVF suddenly declared their support and said they would join in a prison strike. In clashes that followed inside the prison, the UVF and the IRA jointly barricaded themselves in a recreation area and hung two flags from the windows, one the Republican tricolour and the other a white sheet with 'UVF' painted on it. In the street outside, a supporting demonstration of 'loyalists' organised by Mrs Mina Browne reacted to the baffling appearance of the two flags with a novel sound which observers took to be an attempt to cheer and boo at one and the same time. A Vanguard spokesman, with barely concealed disapproval, described the alliance as 'extraordinary', while an Official IRA spokesman in Dublin averred that the UVF prisoners, too, regarded themselves as 'the army of the people'.

By throwing their weight behind the prison strike, Spence and his followers assured it of success, if only because 'loyalists' held most of the 'trusty' jobs in the prison and were therefore in a position to bring its administration to a virtual halt. On 20 June Whitelaw announced concessions which, in effect, accorded both UVF and IRA prisoners political status. The strike was called off, and the hybrid 'people's army' celebrated its shared victory.

Then Spence applied for parole to attend his daughter's wedding. At the best of times, prisoners convicted of murder are not normally granted parole, particularly when less than a third of their sentence has been served. And this was far from the best of times. Spence had just led a prison revolt. Outside, the streets of Belfast were crawling with protestant paramilitary uniforms. And, apparently co-incidentally, Spence's application for parole was for the very weekend on which the UDA had announced its establishment of permanent no-go areas. Nevertheless, parole was approved at ministerial level in

169

the Northern Ireland office and he was freed for forty-eight hours.

Crowds came out to meet and greet him on the Shankill, halting the traffic. He attended the wedding and, according to his own account, spent the evening with his family. Next day he was driven to his mother's house in Joseph Street, and then back to his wife's new home in Springmartin to collect his parole papers prior to his return to jail.

Shortly before six in the evening, he set out for Crumlin Road jail, driven by his sister's son, Frank Curry. As the car turned into Springmartin Road, another pulled in front of it, forcing it into the side. Three men jumped out, wrenched open the door of Spence's car and punched Curry in the face, breaking his nose. When Curry recovered consciousness some five minutes later, Spence and the attackers were gone.

Curry sounded the alarm. The first assumption of the police and the prison authorities was that Spence had been kidnapped by the IRA. When a hooded body was found in a Belfast alley later that night, a police spokesman said it was 'almost certainly Spence', and two national newspapers carried stories of his death next morning.

Then two communiqués arrived at the offices of the *Belfast Telegraph* and Ulster Television. Both were signed 'Captain William Johnston, Adjutant of the UVF'. They claimed that the UVF was holding Spence at a secret hideout 'against his will'. 'When we are certain his case will be reviewed – and if possible another trial agreed upon – then, and only then, will we release him.'

Spence's captors claimed they had tailed him throughout his parole and had made their plans on the Saturday night. Neither Spence nor his family, they said, had any prior knowledge of a rescue attempt. The statement continued:

To the majority of the catholic population we would say:

170

'Unite and join us in defeating the IRA as a means of keeping sectarian warfare from becoming a reality'.

Sectarianism plays no part in our policy and we contend that the working-class people of whatever creed are the real inheritors of peace and prosperity.

Police and army efforts to find Spence were crippled by the UDA's no-go areas on the Shankill, where it was rightly assumed he would be kept. But journalists could move rather more freely, and several joined the search.

He was found by the author, who was leading a British television team. Contact was made through several organisations, including the Red Hand Commandos, and arrangements were made for the TV crew to be blind-folded and driven to meet Spence at a secret destination, which turned out to be one of the many 'loyalist' clubs off the Shankill. The interview that followed, condensed from two hours of film, provided a unique record of source material for the UVF story.

Flanked by a five-man guard armed with sub-machine-guns, Spence denied that he was 'chief of staff' or 'leader' of the UVF, clearly aware of the inconsistency of acknowledging the leadership while also claiming that he was held against his will. He refused to say in what way he had been involved in the UVF in 1966, but he denied having any part in the shooting of Peter Ward. His trial had been 'a farce'. The statements made by McClean and others implicating him had been concocted by the police. The Attorney-General should never have allowed his case to proceed to trial after a lower court had judged there to be insufficient evidence against him.

The UVF, he said, had been active in recent troubles, using its guns 'against anyone who would defy the constitution of Ulster'. He had kept close contact with the force while in prison, but refused to say how. He denied that he had 'run the UVF from a prison cell', but con-firmed that he wished it to play a 'leading role' in the future, 'a much more active role than it has been taking'.

He himself was prepared to 'play any part that fate happens to throw up'.

Asked for his view of the growing number of sectarian assassinations, some of which had been attributed to the UVF, he declared: 'Random killing is to be deplored at any time, and I would say to anyone engaged in sectarian murder "Cease it". If they feel they must become involved in the fight, they should join an appropriate organisation of their choice.'

Spence showed some embarrassment when his letter to Mrs McCann, obtained from her that morning, was read back to him in the presence of his 'captors'. It should not be misconstrued, he said. 'General Irwin Rommel was an honourable soldier and Field Marshal Montgomery gave him respect . . . There's a common bond amongst all honourable soldiers throughout the world.' So it was possible to be an IRA man and to be honourable? 'In exceptions, yes.'

The leaders of the Unionist Party had got the 'loyalist' people into 'one hell of a mess'. It was time 'the people, the small people, the have-nots' took a hand.

One has only to look at the Shankill Road, the heart of the empire that lies torn and bleeding. We have known squalor. I was born and reared in it. No-one knows better than we do the meaning of slums, the meaning of deprivation, the meaning of suffering for what one believes in, whatever the ideology. In so far as people speak of fifty years of misrule, I wouldn't disagree with that. What I would say is this, that we have suffered every bit as much as the people of the Falls Road, or any other underprivileged quarter, in many cases more so.

Asked, finally, to explain the contradiction between his supporters' glorification of his crime and his own denial of it, Spence answered:

What I'm saying is this. I didn't take the actions with which I was charged. I'm not saying I didn't take any actions.

172

Gusty Spence the hero is a myth. The person who sits before you now is truly a humble and sincere man, some people would say misdirected, that is a matter for conjecture. I am sincere in anything I have ever done and I shall be sincere in anything I ever do. But as far as the hero bit's concerned, it's nonsense.

If Spence had given nothing away about the organisation of the UVF and its relationship with other bodies, he had revealed a lot about Gusty Spence: an intense, quiet-spoken, articulate man, much more impressive than the hordes of hooded fire-breathers from the UDA and the IRA who tumbled over each other in their haste to get in front of the cameras. At three in the morning he said a cordial goodbye to the film crew and, on his own orders, was marched away by his armed guard, pausing first to veto a suggestion that one member of the crew should be kept as a hostage, pending his safe get-away. The crew were then hooded again and driven back to their hotel.

As the police hunt for him was stepped up, the 'loyalist' press dubbed him 'the Orange Pimpernel'. It was soon clear that, back in action, he was presiding over a substantial UVF revival. The force's structure of 'divisions', 'companies' and 'battalions' was formalised for the first time. A uniform of leather jackets and army-style black berets was adopted. But hand in hand with this expansion went a number of damaging arrests. Sixteen men were arrested on arms charges and two UVF officers, James Irvine and Thomas Cull, along with two 'volunteers', James Strutt and Norman Sayers, were jailed for six years for an armed robbery in which £509 was stolen for UVF funds. (Cull, incidentally, made a spectacular jail-break two months later). A strange feature of this case was the way in which the four prisoners copied the IRA technique of refusing to recognise the court. Irvine stated from the dock: 'As volunteers in the UVF we refuse to recognise this court as it is an instrument of an illegal and unde-mocratic regime . . . We look upon it as being a continuation of the duplicity which removed our trust in the Stormont parliament. Whitelaw's regime is illegal, if not in law then surely in the eyes of the Lord.'

A more bizarre example of IRA influence on UVF thinking was a project to run a UVF taxi service through the Shankill, where corporation buses had been halted by the no-go areas. A similar IRA service, 'People's Taxis', was operating successfully on the Falls. A UVF spokesman announced that the taxis would 'come under the auspices of the Ulster Volunteer Force, which has a public conscience and a duty to the working people.' A fleet of four cars, soon increased to twenty, ran for several weeks, charging a maximum fare of 10p. The service lasted until buses were put back on the road again later in the year.

There are indications that Spence did not have it all his own way in the higher councils of the UVF. His new emphasis on social concerns was probably incomprehensible to many of his followers, and his opposition to sectarian murders and attacks on catholic areas convinced some that their idol had feet of clay. Restraint was the more difficult to impose since many of the UVF's new wave of recruits were UDA men disenchanted with its lack of 'front line' action. They expected better from the UVF. When they didn't get it, some decided, about the middle of August, to break away and form a group called the Militants. In a paper called *Ulster Militant* in mid-September, the dissidents explained that they represented a number of isolated groups throughout the North which did not believe in defence, but attack:

Most of us, with the exception of two groups, were at one time members of all the other organisations, but we got sick and tired of training with only a general idea of what we were supposed to be training for. We wanted action and we were not allowed to have any. It was always 'tomorrow'.

Gradually, through a contact man, we were convinced that a number of small groups, basically unknown to each other for security reasons but co-operating in attacks on known

174

enemies, would be a more effective weapon against the IRA/Provos and their 'passive' sympathisers. This idea was tried out and proved very successful. But the success was undoubtedly dependent upon anonymity. While the contact men – there are now three – know each other, they are unable to contact their own group leaders. The leaders do the contacting. . . . People who can carry out an attack on a target and remain silent are few and far between, yet any other type, until the Loyalists openly go on the streets, are dangerous to us. . . . Our motto is simple but very apt: *volens et valens,* which means 'willing and able'.

It was possibly this group which planted a car bomb beside Unity Flats on 26 September, killing one resident and injuring twenty-three.

There was dissidence of a different kind in the UDA which, after establishing its permanent no-go areas at the end of June, was clearly at a loss to know what to do next. When the shaky truce between the army and the Provisionals ended in renewed shooting on 10 July, the UDA and Vanguard announced different strategies for forcing the government to act against the IRA. Vanguard announced a 'loyalist' rent and rates strike, UDA a day of mourning on which labour would be withdrawn from all works – including those owned and managed by Vanguard's officers. The UDA attacked Vanguard for an 'ill-conceived and ill-timed move which would only hurt the ordinary working-class people, who will have to pay back the money in the end.' Vanguard, in turn, ostentatiously refused to support the UDA's strike call. The result was that the rent strike was attempted only in country areas, where Vanguard branches were stronger than the UDA, while the day of mourning made little impact outside Belfast, where the UDA was dominant.

The dispute reflected the intensifying leadership battle between the middle-class, conservative Vanguard chiefs and the working-class leaders of the UDA. Craig and his closest lieutenants, still working within the traditional Orange-Unionist framework of party and lodge, were

175

intensely suspicious of independent working-class action, which they saw as crude and communistic. The UDA and LAW were the first explicitly working-class-led bodies to develop wholly within the 'loyalist' community but independently of right-wing official Unionist patronage.

The split looked to be irreparable when Billy Hull announced on 1 August that LAW, after consultations with the UDA (with which, in any case, it was so closely linked as to be, in effect, the Association's political wing), was considering the formation of a new working-class 'loyalist' party aiming at 'government of the people, by the people and for the people, and one man one vote.' But Craig was an old campaigner who knew when to appear to concede defeat while still contriving to keep one finger within trigger's reach. Vanguard would throw its own weight behind a new party, he promised, if it became clear that the Unionist Party could not be captured from within. LAW put its plans for a new party in cold storage – Hull was, after all, a deputy leader of Vanguard – and the UDA was forced to follow suit. It contented itself with an angry swipe at 'the middle-class, self-appointed Unionists leading Vanguard,' and asked: 'Do they realise that the people of Ulster are never again going to be swayed by fine speeches and sabre-rattling?'

But barely three weeks later Vanguard and the UDA were together again, under Craig's leadership. This closing of ranks followed a new outbreak of fighting between the UDA and the army, much the worst yet seen. By now the army had finally invaded and cleared the catholic no-go areas in 'Operation Motorman', but the 'loyalists' had quickly found a new source of frustration: Whitelaw's refusal to invite the UDA or LAW to his forthcoming all-party conference. On 7 September, after a week of mounting violence, the 1st Battalion, Parachute Regiment broke into and searched a UDA 'command post' in Wilton Street, where they found bomb-making equipment. As they left they were fired on, and firing back, they killed two protestants. In the pitched battle that followed, both UDA chairman Jim Anderson and vice-chairman Tommy Herron were taken into custody, and claimed to see a number of their members beaten up by troops before being released. The UDA 'broke off diplomatic relations' with the army, adding for good effect that 'the brutality of the paras has to be seen to be believed. These men are animals and should be taken off the streets of Ulster and sent to the jungle.' A week later UDA and LAW, seeking strength in unity, joined as partners with Vanguard in Craig's new United Loyalist Front. But as if to underline the UDA's continuing class independence, chairman Anderson said in a newspaper interview: 'People are beginning to "catch on" about the Unionist government. The ordinary man is starting to think for himself about the fifty years of misrule that he did have.'

This was an echo of Spence's television interview, and for a time the UVF and the UDA drew more closely together. A joint press statement from both organisations on 14 September warned 'freelance gangsters' that they would be severely dealt with if caught. Three days later, UVF and UDA units were involved in joint action against a catholic estate at Larne. One man, Sinclair Johnson, son of a local UDA leader, was shot dead. Death notices in next day's *Belfast Newsletter* described him as 'sergeant, intelligence unit, East Antrim UVF'. But UDA vice-chairman Tommy Herron, aware of the dangers of public association with a proscribed organisation, was at pains to discountenance rumours of a link-up. 'The UDA and the UVF remain two separate entities,' he insisted, 'and we have no connections at all with one another.'

At the end of September, more rifts opened up. Anderson said in a newspaper interview that his personal choice as 'loyalist' leader was Ian Paisley. He was attacked for this in a statement which purported to have the support of 138 UDA members in the Woodvale, Oldpark, Crumlin and Shankill districts. Herron was also attacked for his 'remarks on providing protection for Roman Catholics and looking after their social needs when the overwhelming majority of protestants are more in need of protection'.

A few days after this jab from the right came another from the left. A circular distributed to the press on 14 October claimed that 'socialist-orientated and class-conscious members of the UDA' were forming 'active service units of the Ulster Citizen Army' for the protection of protestant working-class areas. 'Growing dissatisfaction, frustration and anger within UDA ranks' was 'the result of the increasing influence of Vanguard leadership and ex-Unionist politicians upon the UDA command. These parasites, who never in the past were the friend of the Ulster worker, have not changed. Their sole aim is still pursuit of power at any price.' The new 'active service units' would remain on the alert 'until the UDA clearly shows what they really defend – the Ulster worker or the right of the ruling class to rule.'

Gusty Spence seems to have remained aloof from these faction fights, but not wholly silent. A series of statements issued from 'UVF Brigade Headquarters', mostly condemning the 'hideous crimes' of the sectarian assassins (now running at a murder a day) or other forms of free-lance violence, including 'robberies in the honourable name of the Ulster Volunteer Force'. Another statement poured scorn on Sinn Fein president Tomas MacGiolla for daring to speak in the name of a united working class. 'Has it not been the IRA who have created the strife and the alienation among all the working-class people? Has it not been the activities of the IRA that have resulted in the formation of the UDA and the enormous recruitment in the ranks of the UVF? So, MacGiolla, get your priorities right. You are no more interested in the working-class protestant than the man in the moon!'

The police were still looking for Spence. On 11 October,

three months after his 'abduction', they raided a club off the Shankill after receiving a tip that he was there. Fifty-nine people were arrested and screened, and word spread that Gusty had been lifted. Another night of rioting began on the Shankill. Then in the early hours of the morning it was announced that the man police thought was Gusty was his brother William. The UVF leader was still at large.

But on his release, William Spence told a very different story. According to him, Gusty had indeed been among the fifty-nine arrested. He had been interrogated by police, among them some of the detectives who had been on the Malvern Street murder case. He had then been handed over to the army, but had succeeded in talking himself out of custody, even explaining away identifying tattoos of his daughter's name on his hands.

SDLP MP Paddy Devlin was quick to suggest a conspiracy between the security forces and the UVF. One can only guess at whether William Spence's story was true or simply fodder for the myth-making machine. What Mr Spence never bothered to explain was why, if Gusty was being held by the UVF against his will, he did not take this golden opportunity of giving himself up and returning to jail.

But the news that Gusty was free after all did nothing to quell the riot on the Shankill: riots have a momentum impervious to logic. By the weekend virtually the whole of protestant working-class Belfast, east and west of the river, was in a state of siege. When an army vehicle rammed a UDA volunteer against a wall, killing him, Tommy Herron declared that the UDA was at war with the army. 'To hell with the British army! To hell with the Whitelaw administration! What future has Northern Ireland from an administration whose troops kill people like this in cold blood? The British army and the British government are now our enemies.'

In the '48-hour war' that followed there were sustained

gun battles – the heaviest Belfast had seen, even at the height of the Provisional offensive – between troops and UDA units all over the city. Four civilians were killed and more than a hundred troops and police treated for gunshot wounds. 'We are not heading for civil war, we are in that state already,' pronounced Paisley.

Then as suddenly as it began the firing stopped. The UDA council met senior army officers and agreed a truce. Herron emerged to tell the waiting press: 'Our war with the army is over. Both sides will now do all in their power to take the heat out of the situation . . . I believe that 99 per cent of the army are perfect gentlemen'. The ambivalence of 'loyalist' militants towards the Queen's forces had never been more strikingly demonstrated since protestant gunmen had shot dead PC Arbuckle on the Shankill exactly three years earlier.

The UVF was quick to deny any part in the UDA's war. 'It is not our policy to shoot at British troops,' declared 'Captain William Johnston'. But it was not standing idly by. At 4.15 on the morning of 23 October, fourteen UVF men, dressed in army uniforms, held up the sentry at Lurgan UDR and Territorial Army depot, forcing their way inside at gun point. There they demanded the keys of the armoury, but the duty guard locked himself inside and refused to open the door until the UVF threatened to shoot a number of guardroom hostages one by one. When the door was opened the raiders seized eighty-three self-loading rifles, twenty-one sub-machineguns and 1,300 rounds of ammunition, hijacking an army Land Rover to carry it all away. Part of the haul was dumped in a derelict cottage nearby, the raiders having taken more than they could cope with.

Within hours, catholic leaders voiced the suspicion that the raid was a put-up job, arranged between the UVF and extremist members of the UDR. These suspicions were fed by the frequency with which UDR men were reporting the theft of weapons from their homes, and by the growing number of cases before the courts in which UDR men faced firearms charges. On 22 October, British Defence Minister of State, Lord Balniel, admitted in the Commons that plain-clothes army patrols had been involved in twenty shooting incidents, fuelling NICRA charges that the army's SAS murder squad was active on the 'loyalist' side. On 26 October the UDR commander declared that there was no ban on UDA membership in his regiment, despite the fact that the UDR was a component part of the army with which the UDA had fought a forty-eight-hour war earlier that month, and on 1 November Bernadette Devlin complained that a Corporal Tyler of the army's Military Intelligence (Special Investigations Branch) had been mysteriously transferred to England before completing an investigation into collusion between the UDR and the UDA.

Meanwhile, its war with the British army in abeyance, the UDA took a decision to carry its offensive over the border into the Republic. On 5 October it claimed that a detachment had seized rifles and explosives in an IRA arms dump in county Monaghan. A week later Billy Hull told a Vanguard rally in Bangor that they were now taking the war south of the border. On 1 November four UDA men bombed a bar in St Johnstown, county Donegal, and the organisation warned southern bar-owners that 'action would be taken against all premises that harbour the scum of the IRA'. Five days later a soft drinks factory on the Donegal side of the border was blown up in retaliation for an IRA blast in Londonderry. On 7 November the Vanguard council formally approved the UDA's border raids and expressed the hope that they would help the Dublin government take action against the IRA.

On 13 November an army patrol discovered a bomb factory in protestant Dee Street, Belfast, where they recovered three quarters of a ton of explosive mixture, one of the biggest hauls since the emergency began. The bombings south of the border went on, and twenty-five

181

people were injured in a cinema blast in Dublin on 26 November. At first it was assumed to be the work of the Provisionals, protesting at the conviction of Seán Mac Stiofáin, but when two men were killed and 127 injured in two more blasts in the city on 1 December, serving only to give Jack Lynch a timely hand in getting his new anti-IRA laws through the Dáil, suspicions turned on the northern protestants. The UDA and the UVF both denied this one, and the mystery deepened when a member of the British secret service was arrested a few days later. Three more bombs exploded in the south on 28 December, killing a fifteen-year-old girl and a sixteen-year-old boy. The UDA again denied responsibility, as did both wings of the IRA.

Spence was by now back in Crumlin Road jail. On 4 November he was spotted not far from his home in Springmartin by a patrol of the 1st Battalion, Parachute Regiment. The battalion commander claimed that his men had been watching the area for weeks, and that he had acted on a hunch that Spence would be in the car in which he was picked up. But the army press officer described it as a purely fortuitous arrest. Spence was alone and put up no resistance. Still sticking to the story that he had been held by the UVF against his will, he blandly claimed that he had 'just evaded his captors'.

1972 ended with a new flare-up of ideological warfare within the UDA. Early in October an army patrol had stopped a car containing 'Duke' Ernie Elliott, 'Lieutenant-Colonel' of Woodvale. Searching the car, they found manuals on urban guerilla warfare and literature on Trotsky, Franz Fanon and Che Guevara. On 7 December, Elliott was found shot dead not far from his home, and the RUC made it known that they did not suspect the IRA. It was widely concluded, though without firm evidence, that Elliott, having identified himself with a left faction within the UDA, had been killed by a faction of the right.

Six weeks later, Elliott's first-in-command, David Fogel, defected from the UDA and sold his story to the *Sunday Times*. He attacked Harding Smith for proposing a formal link-up between the UDA and the UVF, dismissed Craig as 'in it for himself', described Unionist politicians as 'middle-class smartie-pants poncing down our streets once every five years asking for our votes and then never bothering to come again until the next election', and finally expressed the hope that some day the UDA and the Official IRA would get together 'because both organisations have the working people at heart'.

1972 had been a grim year. 1973 promised little better. Once again the New Year saw Ulster waiting for Heath's package, to be wrapped in a White Paper spelling out the government's proposals for the future government of Northern Ireland. This much could be safely predicted: Whitelaw would reject a United Ireland without protestant consent, but he would also set his face against a return to Stormont with its own security powers. That would leave Ulster a glorified county council. Such a package would never be acceptable to the IRA: could it be made acceptable to the 'loyalists'? Faulkner and Paisley, in unaccustomed alliance, would cry 'betrayal!' – but would eventually choose acceptance rather than civil war, arguing that only the ultimate betrayal of a United Ireland could justify a protestant insurrection. Craig, some of the UDA, and some of the UVF, would cry 'betrayal! ' – and mean it. 'Moderate' would do battle with 'extremist', but the old battle would have new and complex overtones of class and ideology. There would be no nice, clear-cut decision; no Armageddon, but no peace either. Ulster would stay poised on the edge of the abyss: but, as a Stormont official was reported as saying when the Provisionals resumed their bombing campaign in January, the abyss keeps moving.

11 THE FUTURE

What, then, is the social role of the UVF, in all its varied forms?

The historical role of Orangeism is clear. From its inception at the end of the eighteenth century, the Order marshalled protestant peasants and artisans behind the political interests of the ruling ascendancy class. It did so quite consciously, almost cynically. Protestant tenants and employees were induced by sectarian manipulation to back the political interests of their landlords and employees, even though those interests were diametrically opposed to their own. Thus the Order marshalled protestant workers against every proposal to extend the franchise, and, indeed, against virtually every progressive measure enacted by a parliament under pressure to contain the forces of democracy. Orangeism was essentially an ideology of counter-revolution.

In addition to the potent weapon of sectarianism, the Order made ample use of the whole repertoire of mystification by which workers elsewhere in the British Isles were side-tracked from pursuit of their own class interests so that they lined up behind those who exploited them. These mystifications were labelled 'Crown', 'Country', 'Empire', 'Patriotism', 'Loyalty' and 'Law and Order', concepts more explosive than gunpowder, and much more effective in the defence of minority rule.

Carson's UVF was the armed mobilisation of a section of the working class behind the Belfast commercial and business elite whose economic and political dominance was threatened by a democratic solution to the Irish problem. It was Europe's first distinctively fascist movement: Mussolini was to organise a similarly motivated armed mobilisation of the 'lumpenproletariat' in Italy, and Hitler in Germany. Since 'fascism' has become a crude and almost meaningless word of abuse, flung indiscriminately at more or less every shade of opinion in Irish politics, it is as well to remind ourselves that the term has a quite specific meaning which can only be grasped within a framework of class politics. Fascism is not violence, or racism, or jingoism, or authoritarianism, or corporativism, though it draws on all these. It is the ideology by which a threatened ruling class mobilises and arms a backward, lumpen element of the working class against that section of workers which, by its pursuit of democracy, threatens bourgeois ascendancy.

By this definition, the only one which makes historical sense, the Unionist Party itself is seen to have played at least a quasi-fascist role throughout most of its history, both in persuading protestant workers to back their bosses against their fellow-workers, and, crucially, in arming them to smash the opposition. Reaction was victorious in 1920 when the British government thought to solve the Irish problem by partitioning Ireland into two client states, an act which thwarted the clearly expressed will of the majority for Irish independence, and enthroned the anti-democratic principle of minority rule. For fifty years thereafter, Northern Ireland was governed by a coalition of the old ascendancy class and that section of the working class which opposed democratic majority rule in a united Ireland.

But this coalition was inherently unstable. The common label 'protestant' confers only an illusory unity on the Shankill Road stager and the pedigree planter in the Big House. Behind that illusory unity is a profound disunity of class interests. The gentlemen who ran the Unionist Party were always ready to discourage any distinctive working-class consciousness, since they were very well aware that, while 'protestants' outnumbered 'catholics', workers far outnumbered gentlemen.

So anachronistic and reactionary a system could hold together only as long as Ulster remained isolated from the main current of British politics, with its hazy but unmistakable class alignments, and so long as the silent majority of the Irish people, the catholics or nationalists, north and south, stayed silent. By the mid-'sixties neither condition applied, and the perverse social contract between protestant workers and the Unionist leadership began to come under mounting strain.

When the UVF began to kill catholics in 1966 and Paisley's and Bunting's Volunteers attacked civil rights marchers in 1968, they were acting out the traditional role of the ascendancy class's bully-boys. It was a natural reflex in times of trouble. But the Unionist leadership could no longer afford to approve or condone such reflexes since its survival had come to depend less on lumpen support at home than on approval from Westminster. So the UVF was proscribed and Paisleyism denounced as fascism. The result was an unprecedented rift in the coalition of classes on which Unionist supremacy was dependent, with Paisley heading up a new working-class Unionism.

Clearly the rift arose from tactical, not social differences: the protestant working class broke with O'Neill because he was soft on catholics, not because he left protestant workers in slum houses. But the social chemistry of the situation was such that, once a rift *had* opened up, the protestant working class began to become aware of specific class issues. They began, slowly, to develop a class consciousness. And they began to feel their strength as a class, distinctive and separate from middle-class Unionists.

The battle then began between those (like Craig and Faulkner) who sought to reimpose the traditional coalition of classes, in which the working class served the interests of the ruling elite, and those (like Paisley and Boal) who chose to try and create a new Unionism based on the protestant working class alone. That battle continues to rage in 1973, and may well prove no less significant (and possibly no less bloody) than the sectarian war on the streets.

It is fashionable in Northern Ireland affairs to talk of scenarios. There is a malign and a benign scenario for the protestant working class.

The malign scenario entails a reimposition of traditional alignments. Either under the Unionist Party or the Vanguard label, the UDA, UVF and associated bodies unite behind Craig in resistance to a new, imposed constitution. The protestant working class is once again used by its masters, its class enemies, unrecognised as such, to maintain the protestant ascendancy. Northern Ireland's politics remain calcified on unreal sectarian, rather than real class, lines. In one form or another, the age-old war goes on.

The benign scenario supposes that, having once begun, even tentatively, to strike out on its own, the protestant working class will choose to make its own politics. It develops a tradition of working-class leadership. It discovers that the Unionist old guard, if it is to be defeated, must be challenged not only on 'loyalist' issues but on economic issues too. It rediscovers the identity of interest it has with the catholic working class in transforming a protestant state for protestant people into a workers' state for working-class people, and in doing so discovers an identity of interest with the democratic movement in the south.

Preposterously optimistic? Maybe. But who, when the latest troubles began, would have dared prophesy Paisley's realignments: his discovery, for instance, of the shared social goals of his Democratic Unionist Party and the catholic Social-Democratic and Labour Party? Who, when Gusty Spence led the UVF into action in 1966, could have foreseen his condemnation, in 1972, of 'fifty years of Unionist misrule', and his bitter acknowledgement that the Shankill had been conned into believing it had a part in the ascendancy? Who, when Billy Hull marched with Craig to those first Vanguard rallies, could have predicted that within months he would be talking of a 'workers' party' based on the civil rights marchers' principle, 'one man one vote'? Who, when the UDA first appeared on the streets of Belfast early in 1972, could have known that before the year was out a faction within it would be publicly demanding 'more socialist-orientated policies', and even a tie-up with the Marxist-influenced Official IRA?

In the malign scenario, the UDA and UVF will allow themselves to be used to impose, once again, a form of fascism on Northern Ireland, with or without Britain's connivance. In the benign scenario, they are the agency by which Orange fascism is finally discredited and defeated, bringing about conditions in which it is at last possible to envisage the beginning of the end of Ireland's British problem.

January 28 1973.